Sacred Union

A Journey to Joyful Living

Written By

Suzanna Kennedy

Published By

Reality Crafting

Sacred Union: **A Journey to Joyful Living**

Copyright © 2006 Reality Crafting

Written by Suzanna Kennedy
Cover Art by Suzanna Kennedy
Front cover photograph by Tanya Ferguson
Waterfall photograph by Suzanna Kennedy
Wedding picture by Connie Anderson

Reality Crafting
P.O. Box 732
Kapaa, HI 96746
Toll Free in the U.S. 866 363-9001
Hawaii Direct: 808 821-1393
www.realitycrafting.com
Email: sacredunion@realitycrafting.com

Dedication

This book is dedicated to all my creations
I love you
I give you life
I give you freedom of expression
May you bless
All That Is

Suzanna Kennedy

Contents

Acknowledgements

I wish to acknowledge the **family of my youth**: my parents, George and Bernie, my sister, Michele, my brothers, Frank and Rob. Your love, your support and your unique expressions of spirit were the delicious flavoring in the chicken soup of my soul. You co-created the perfect environment for me to seek and discover my purpose. By your examples, I found the courage to live it.

Family of my heart: my son, James and my daughter, Angela. You were both such a joy to have and to hold in my arms and in my heart. The two of you are sacred reflections, mirroring the polar opposite expressions of me. James, your boundless creative expressions never cease to amaze me. Your vision, your passion and your leadership lights the way for many as we co-create Paradise on Earth. Angela, I admire your beauty, your tender heart, your centeredness and your willingness to step in and get the job done. You speak your truth — not an easy thing to do in this world.

Family of my soul: Kathy Lowe, a dear soul sister who has seen me through all of the passages written in this book. She was my mentor in the corporate world and now serves on my Creative Team, helping me to share *Sacred Union* teachings with the world. Her guidance and support along the way has been the rudder on my ship through unknown waters. Jeanne Nicholson — what a ride it has been! Your daily emotional and spiritual support has helped me to ground this book in the physical world. You have been the first one I called when I needed help — and you were always there for me. You were the first one I called when there was something to celebrate because we won the victory together.

I'd like to thank all of my **students**. I have learned much from you. Every one of you is a beacon of light, radiating in all directions. I am honored by the trust you laid at my feet. It has been a pleasure to serve as your spiritual midwife. Thank you for your courage and commitment to our Divine Plan to co-create Paradise on Earth. We're doing it!

Casey, my beloved *Sacred Union Partner* — I love you. I love you. I love you. Thank you for showing up when I called to you. Thank you for continuing to show up every day. Thank you for your courage. Thank you for your integrity. Thank you for nurturing me with your tender heart. And thank you for nourishing me with your light. Thank you for allowing me to behold your magnificent beauty, both inside and out. Thank you for being my guardian and protector. Because of you, *Sacred Union* continues to spread out in concentric circles around the globe. Soon we will feel the ripple of our own love coming back to us through smiling hearts of those we serve together.

Foreword

By Alan Cohen

While many people on the planet are going through (sometimes intense) changes, the changes you are going through are not random. They are an intrinsic part of your soul's process of awakening. What could be more important?

Suzanna Kennedy went through some dramatic changes that appeared quite strange to people who viewed her from her then-life as a traditional wife and corporate consultant. If she were to cling to that life out of fear, you would not be reading this book today. Yet Suzanna found the courage and trust to breathe through her transformation and utter a bold "Yes!" to the Phoenix rising from the ashes of the outworn.

Part One will take you through the corridors of the mind and heart, and highlight for you the core principles of Suzanna's *Sacred Union* teachings. If I could sum up Suzanna's message, she is shouting to us, "You can take charge of your life and really live your dreams!" Most important, her methods are anchored in the divine. This journey has a completely spiritual foundation, yet it honors the physical path as an expression of the sacred. And there is no more powerful context in which to hold your life. You are a spiritual being on a physical adventure. *Divine Human Upgrades* will help you to remember who you are and lift your life to your highest purpose.

In the second part of the book Suzanna shares her amazing journey from who she was to who she is. As I read her fascinating account, it occurred to me that who she is becoming is who we are all becoming. We are moving from the dark, heavy, and limited, to the light, free, and divine. Sometimes we have no idea how this is happening, but it is. Sometimes the weirdest and least sensible experiences form the strongest pillars of our new life. As you read Suzanna's story, you will likely recognize your own. Suzanna's gift is to show you a vision of the wonderful realm to which you are heading.

While Suzanna recounts her visits to many countries and exotic destinations from Sedona to Egypt, she is describing less a physical travelogue and more a journey of consciousness. While we believe we are traveling the earth, we are really traveling the terrain of the soul. One of Suzanna's great talents is to recognize the spiritual elements of a physical journey, and extract esoteric lessons where others would be distracted by appearances.

Suzanna's website is called *Reality Crafting* and that is exactly what she is teaching here. Indeed we are all crafting our reality in every moment. Our great need is to do this *consciously*, by choice, from the heart, in co-creation with Spirit. That is exactly what you will find out how to do in *Sacred Union*.

I wish there were more teachers like Suzanna Kennedy on the planet. She is a shining model of transformation from the inside out, and living from deliberate creation rather than default. I take great satisfaction in knowing that she is teaching and inspiring you to do the same.

Blessings on your great journey. May you find *divinity* within your own soul, and express it in all your relationships wherever you travel.

Radiant One

We have it then — in the beginning there was you. You are light. You are a Radiant Being of golden light, shining brightly. Brighter than any star. Bright as a Radiant Child of God. You are Light and to Light you shall return. Be confident in your radiance, dear one. Be alive in the light. Be the light. Shine. It's what you are. It is all you have to do. The time of doing is over. Your radiance has been seen by all the other beings of light, and they are attracted to you. They honor you, you Divine Radiant being.

Whence you came from the light? You came to experience yourself as a Creator God. You came to play with form. You clothed yourself in a body of matter. It was dense and heavy, and you adjusted to that in time. But once anchored in the density, you began to forget from whence you came. You forgot to remember your radiance. You entered the three-dimensional earth hologram and agreed to play the game.

Radiant One, it is time to remember who you really are. It is time to shine on the world once more. It is time to let your profound love flow through you to teach and heal. It is time, dear one. It is time.

Whole nations grew up around the notion of one God, one Supreme Being. Nations, not only on this planet and this dimension, but many others as well. What is God then? God is all. God is pure energy. God is all. The totality. The light and the dark together. The good and the bad together. There is no light or dark. There is no good or bad. There is only God. You are God expressing through a human body now. Your personality is like a role you play in a movie. It is not who you are. It is not fixed. Does every actor in a movie become that role for the rest of their life? No.

You are not your personality. You are not your thoughts. You are not your beliefs. You are not your feelings. You are not your behaviors. You are God expressing the creative life force through a human body, choosing to focus your attention through the physical eyes and perspective of that one physical body at a time. But all other physical bodies are God too. They are you too. In the denseness of form, you forgot that.

So your purpose now, in this time, on this planet, is to remember who you really are. It is to bring your radiance into this body. It is to transmute this dense physical body into a body of Light. It is to anchor spirit into matter and express Heaven on Earth.

Each body will express spirit and create heaven in a unique way. Oh the magnificence of this Divine plan. How many ways can we express Heaven on Earth? There's a different Heaven for every body. Can you imagine that?

I wrote *Radiant One* in the fall of 2000 while still living in Sedona, Arizona. At the time, I had been facilitating clearing sessions for about two years. I kept getting hints from Spirit, through various psychic readers, about a book that I was supposed to write.

The psychics couldn't tell me what the book should be about, so I decided to sit down and pretend it was already written. Perhaps I could open up a conduit to the already-written, future book and let it dictate itself to me. I sat down in front of the computer screen, facing a blank page, said a prayer, got quiet and just listened. What I heard, in its entirety, was the words of *Radiant One*. It came through clearly, intact, in one short sitting. I never edited a word.

The energy that came through with the words was so strong, my hands shook and tears rolled down my cheeks — every cell seemed electrified. Later I understood that it was an intense energy transmission. I didn't write another word for a whole year. It took me that long to integrate the energy of the transmission. And I knew that before I could write another word, I had to BE the *Radiant One* I wrote of.

During that year I shed many layers of the onion of who I believed myself to be. My spiritual guidance was strong and it led me to spend a month on Kaua'i, three weeks in Egypt, back to Kaua'i, two months touring Europe and then a permanent move from Sedona to Kaua'i.

When the creative juices began to flow again, instead of a book, the *Sacred Union Technology* was born. I was given an integrated series of initiations. The *Sacred Union Technology* is "how to" become the *Radiant One*. This book, written after I have facilitated hundreds of *Sacred Union* initiations, is the story about how the *Sacred Union Technology* came into being, how it works, and why it works. Now that I have embodied *Sacred Union* myself, I can transmit the initiations in a multitude of ways, including through this book itself.

The purpose of this book is to invite you to begin your journey into *Sacred Union* with your own Divine Self. It is to transmit the initiations, if you wish to receive them. And to let you know that there are a growing number of *Divine Human*s co-creating Paradise on Earth. We call you to join us.

On this journey, the road is one of courage, as you let go of the structure of the fear-based belief matrix that you've shared with mass consciousness for so long. It isn't always easy to have faith in the new love-based matrix. Especially when there are so few people to look to for evidence that it really exists. It takes courage and a strong will to focus on what you want to create instead of allowing your attention to be grabbed by the abundant and insistent illusions of fear, lack and separation.

If I can do it, so can you. My gift to you is that I forged a new road. I wandered around, up blind alleys, into dead ends, in circles and out again, until I found it. Then I went back and marked the straightest path. I paved the way. For you it will be easier, faster, more conscious and graceful than it was for me. Allow me to be your navigator. You are in the driver's seat. Together we can arrive, just in time, back home, to YOU — *Radiant One.*

Part One

The Technology

Upgrade Your Life

Your DNA is an elegant, sophisticated computer program consisting of two versions. The basic code contains 3% of the total, which has been mapped by scientists to our current biology. The other 97% (referred to as junk DNA by genetic scientists) are in hidden files, lying dormant.

Within the hidden files is a completely upgraded version of the human being. It features 12 strands of DNA instead of two. Along with the extra 10 strands comes many new features and abilities, that from the viewpoint of a 2-strand being could be considered **Divine.**

Divine .....

1. Having the nature of or being a deity.

2. Of, relating to, emanating from, or being the expression of a deity.

3. Superhuman; godlike.

4. Supremely good or beautiful; magnificent.

5. Heavenly; perfect.

6. Relating to, or proceeding directly from God or a god.

This hidden upgrade is being activated, installing itself like a *Microsoft Automatic Update.*

Some individuals have been already activated by the increasing sunspot activity, celestial energy infusing the planet, and energy coming from Mother Earth herself. All humans will be activated at some point. There are twelve activation waves. First-wave individuals, like me, are nearly complete with their upgrades and are among the facilitators who are helping the next waves come on-line.

Discover how to accelerate the integration of the upgrades and how to use the new features that are coming on-line. When you become conscious and attuned to the upgrade, integration is faster and more graceful. This gives you access to the new features sooner.

If you are reading this, you are ready for activation and/or attunement and training in how to use the new features of the upgrade. This information will not register with those who are not ready.

The new features of the *Divine Human Upgrade* will upgrade all areas of your life: mental, emotional, spiritual and physical. The ultimate result of the upgrades is **Sacred Union Consciousness**.

Upgraded Mental Features

- Upgraded self-identity (ego)
- Uninstall social control programming
- Access universal wisdom and knowledge outside your experience
- Release connection between painful memories and unexpressed emotional energy
- Release victimhood
- Access higher guidance
- Ability to see beyond the illusion
- Upgrade your discernment skills
- Upgrade your personal integrity
- Upgrade your authenticity
- Upgrade your communication skills

Upgraded Emotional Features

- Release past, hidden, unexpressed emotional energy
- Upgrade your ability to process emotional material
- Upgrade your ability to forgive

- Upgrade your ability to trust
- Upgrade your capacity for intimacy
- Upgrade your capacity for compassion

Upgraded Physical Features

- Bring body into healthful balance
- Release disease programs
- Increase longevity
- Activate rejuvenation program

Upgraded Spiritual Features

- Activate and read your Divine Plan (soul's purpose)
- Remember alternate incarnations
- Transcend Karma
- Establish communication with higher aspects of your being
- Establish communication of other-dimensional beings
- Multi-dimensional travel: time, bi-locate, teleport
- Upgrade multi-dimensional senses
- Upgrade your manifesting abilities

Sacred Union

When I first heard the words *Sacred Union,* it resonated with me as a name for a kind of relationship that my heart yearned for, but my mind couldn't quite describe. It's a relationship whose blueprint must come from another universe where joy, love and freedom reign. It seems like a relationship that doesn't exist here yet, but maybe something we could evolve to.

To me *Sacred Union* described coming together in pure, unconditional love, sharing deep intimacy and passion, allowing for complete freedom to be, to grow and to change. It's feeling free to be *Who You Really Are* with no masks, illusions or projections. It's got to be better than our contemporary institution of marriage, given the astounding divorce rate. Yet here in Kaua'i, we see scores of wedding and honeymoon couples beginning their union. How many of them will achieve a *Sacred Union*? How many will become disillusioned?

Upon meeting, many couples describe feeling instantly comfortable. They notice a feeling of familiarity, as if they've known each other forever. They may explain this as being soul mates or lovers from another lifetime. Yet usually, after time, this magical feeling is replaced by "the honeymoon is over" kind of feeling.

> "In the presence of love, anything unlike love, presents itself."
>
> Sondra Ray, Author, *Loving Relationships*

Here's what happens. Just when we begin to feel safe and secure in another's love and in the relationship, all of the unloved parts of ourselves present themselves for healing. We all have denied thoughts, beliefs, judgments and suppressed emotions lurking in the closets and under the beds of our psyche. When these disenfranchised parts feel the energy of love, they want to come out and be loved too. They want to be acknowledged, accepted and healed by the love.

But most often when they show themselves, we are repulsed. After all, we spent a lot of emotional energy hiding from them and keeping them hidden from others. How dare they show themselves now, just when everything was going so well!

If we were conscious and aware, we'd recognize this as a wonderful opportunity to heal those denied parts of us into love and light — into wholeness. Yet most of us are not aware of this opportunity, and we banish those denied parts into deeper exile. We may break up with our partner, only to repeat the pattern again in the next relationship. Or we may stay in the relationship, closing off aspects of ourselves that we would rather not face — sacrificing deep intimacy in favor of superficial comfort and safety.

What is ironic is that those denied parts, even though hidden, are usually very instrumental in attracting our partners in the first place. It is those denied parts that provide the feeling of familiarity, because it was those parts that didn't feel loved by our parents. We will attract a partner who will withhold love in the same kind of way that we perceived that our parents withheld love. Those denied parts move us to set up similar situations over and over again so that we will finally look at the denial and love it into the light.

So how do we get off this merry-go-round? How can we love ourselves into the light so that we don't have to play this out in relationship? How can we heal our broken hearts and open to the intimacy of *Sacred Union*? These are questions I asked my spiritual guides. They responded to my questions in the most profound and tangible way.

They told me that they could bring me a *Sacred Union* partner if I made two agreements. First, I must be willing to go through the deep transformation necessary to come into *Sacred Union* within myself. Then, and only then, I would attract a *Sacred Union* partner. Second, once I had that partner, they wanted me to teach others how to journey into their own *Sacred Union*.

I did not hesitate to agree. Thus my journey to *Sacred Union* began. You can read about it later in this book. In a nutshell, the journey led me back to myself — yet an expanded view of Self —

as a *Divine Human*. From this reunion with my Divinity, which I enjoyed alone for several months, I called forth a partner to share my new *Divine Human* Self with. Casey showed up to answer my call. With Spirit's side of the bargain fulfilled, it is my great joy and honor to share what I have learned with others who wish to journey into their own *Sacred Union*.

Understand that *Sacred Union* is first and foremost *Sacred Union* within you — all aspects of yourself, in all time, all dimensions. This includes coming into *Sacred Union* with our own Divinity. We must acknowledge, feel and allow our wholeness and oneness with Source. By definition every human is Divine. The human being is the *Sacred Union* of the individualized consciousness of All That Is and physical matter. Humans are the *Sacred Union* of Spirit and Earth. Yet there are varying degrees to which people are aware of their own Divine nature. And there are varying degrees to which people express their Divinity.

As our individual consciousness journeyed into the density of matter, we have felt disconnected from our spiritual source. We have fallen asleep and dreamed that we are separate from our own Divinity. The process used in the *Sacred Union* technology helps you to awaken and clear away the dream of separation. You will rebirth yourself into the world of form with the awakened knowing that you are a *Divine Human,* creating Paradise on Earth.

Since the original emergence from Source, as an individualized Divine Spark, human beings have been re-enacting the Illusion of Separation in all of their relationships. In one way or another, we suffer pain in our interactions with other. Even the most loving relationships end in grief when one person dies before the other. We store the dense energies related to pain and separation in our four-body system (physical, mental, emotional and spiritual body).

It is the separation that we feel that leads us to want to connect in relationship. We mistakenly believe that there is another "soul mate" that can make us whole. We continue to expect others to fill in the holes in the Swiss cheese of our soul. We continue to re-enact separation, abandonment, betrayal and victimhood until we break through the veil of illusion and see that there is no separation from Source, from Self or from each other.

ed Union Consciousness

Activation and integration of the *Divine Human Upgrades* will begin the journey to *Sacred Union Consciousness*. It is this new, evolving being, called a *Divine Human* that can host *Sacred Union Consciousness*.

To better illustrate *Sacred Union Consciousness*, consider this imagery. Imagine that the size of your whole body represents *Who You Really Are* in your totality as a Divine Spark of Source. It is all of you, in all times, all dimensions and all realities.

The self that you are aware of in this body, on this planet, in this lifetime is about the size of the fingernail on your pinky finger.

As you expand into the various levels of *Sacred Union Consciousness,* you become more aware of more of the body. For example, you experience a jump of expanded consciousness and your awareness leaps from knowing yourself as a fingernail to knowing yourself as a whole hand.

With this expansion comes the understanding that you create your own reality by the decisions you make, the intentions you put out and where you focus your attention. You understand that for every decision you make there is an alternate version of you in another dimension playing out the results of a yes decision, when you made a no decision in this dimension. You know and feel that are not separate from Source. You understand that you are an individualized expression of Source (God/Goddess, Creator).

In the next expansion, you may become aware of yourself as a whole arm. But still, the right hand doesn't know what the left hand is doing. That left hand may be an alternate version of you that has decided to explore a lifetime of greed, control, manipulation and abuse of power.

You will continue to expand in leaps and bounds until you come into full consciousness of *Who You Really Are*. But that's not all. At the same time, you are becoming aware that there is no separation between you and Source. There is no separation between you and the other Divine Sparks of Source. Oneness won't be a concept to you anymore. It will be your truth.

Imagine remembering all of the experiences you have had in other dimensions. You remember all the knowledge, the wisdom, the skills you have accumulated in your journeys through creation. You remember creation. You know your power as a Divine Spark of Source. Because you know no separation from All That Is, you wield that power with compassion and wisdom. Imagine all that, while still in human form — *Divine Human* form.

Full consciousness is a wondrous state in which the realms of physical and the spiritual are full merged. You possess psychic talents such as telepathy (thought communicating), telekinesis (ability to move objects through thought), and clairvoyance (ability to see into the future). Moreover, with the inherent gift to vividly see the world of Spirit, you are able to converse freely with your beloved departed ones as well as with the Spiritual Hierarchy. In short, your now latent, Christ-like abilities become full manifested.

Full conscious reality is truly multi-dimensional in form. You need to accept that fully-conscious individuals exist on two levels simultaneously — the personal and the group. In effect, such Beings are a true hologram of the whole as well as a full representation of themselves. Their degree of presence is truly astounding. Moreover, they are filled with grace, compassionate, and a natural understanding of others. They draw upon the wisdom of the ancestors and their own past lives, are in contact with the Spiritual Hierarchy, and are true Physical Angels.

Sheldan Nidle, Author, *Your First Contact*

Planetary Activation

The consciousness of our dear Mother Earth, Gaia, has decided to upgrade and return herself to her original blueprint of Paradise. She was gracious enough to play hostess to the Polarity Integration Game. The game board is three-dimensional and denser than her natural fifth dimensional state.

The Polarity Integration Game is over!!! The key to winning was compassion. In this game, when it is over and complete — we are all winners — there are no losers. Because we realize it was all a game and at different times each of us has played the villain and the hero, the victim and the perpetrator, the master and the slave. We have all explored all the roles in this game, and we are now feeling complete. We can let go of the polarity. No longer do we need to experience fear to know love or pain to know joy. We can choose joy in every moment if we want to.

So the game is over, but not all parts of us know it yet. It is like a chicken with its head cut off. Think of that image for a moment; meditate on it. For it will give you a clue as to what is going to be showing up in this world for the next few years.

A chicken with its head cut off. The chicken in this case is polarity. We know its going to die, but it keeps running around as if it is still alive. If we keep an eye on it, we can avoid getting stepped on. We can just step aside and let it pass. Why does it keep running around — cell memory. Every cell contains a historical library. Watch where it goes, it will return to all of its old stomping grounds. It will try all of its old tricks one more time before it lies down for good.

In this world of polarity, we've had the light and the dark. Of course, within each of us there is light and dark also. Light is love and darkness is the void and it is unknown. We have been taught to fear the unknown. We have sent those denied and unexamined aspects of ourselves away, into the void. We pushed away our fears, our guilt, and our shame. We sent them into the void.

Inside the void, it seems like it is empty, but is really filled with the pure potential of everything. From the void the unexpressed thoughts and emotions take form and emerge, embodied. They take on the role of evil villain, oppressor, tyrant, dictator and play out our worst fears on the screen of our reality.

The dark has been expressing itself as those few men that have been exerting their power through government, finance, education and mass media. Compassion has been flooding the Earth in the past few months. It has been prayed for, delivered and anchored through many light workers all over the planet. It has shifted the consciousness of the planet to a vibration higher than polarity. So those playing the role of the bad guys (this time) will surrender to it. They will allow all the cover-ups to be uncovered. They will allow their lies and manipulations to come into the light. It is only in the light of day that they can be healed. Now they are ready, so they will allow it. It is their Higher Self that will allow it. Their ego self might not agree, so you will see some serious kicking and screaming.

What does that mean for us? As we watch all of the disclosures, it will be quite ugly. There will be rage and resentment within the people. There will be disbelief and disillusionment. Some will feel discouraged and hopeless. For some, it will feel like the rug of their whole belief system is being torn out from under them.

Remember, the chicken is running around with its head cut off and this is only temporary. As soon as it runs out of blood, it will lie down and not be heard from again. This is what we've been waiting for. This is why we all wanted to be here on Earth at this time.

What do we do in the meantime? How can we get through this stage most gracefully? Remember the key is compassion. As we look at the atrocities as they are revealed, we need to have compassion for those who appear to have wronged us. Why? Because they are our mirrors! They are our own dark sides. They are our left hands, while we've been focusing on our right. We asked them to play the part. Yes, they have exaggerated our dark side profusely, but this was necessary for us to see it and recognize it. Otherwise, it would go on forever, easy to deny and overlook. We could nominate them for Academy Awards; they've played the part so well.

Planetary Activation

If you see manipulation in the outside world, look within to see if there is anywhere in your life you use manipulation. If you see lies, look at where you are not telling the truth to yourself or others. If you see greed, recognize it as a fear of lack and look within for your own fear of lack, fear of survival. Bring the ray of compassion into yourself, fill yourself with it, to overflowing and then send it to the "bad guys". Then begin coming into integrity with yourself.

Don't buy into the fear. There will be massive fear-based propaganda unleashed. This has already begun. I repeat, don't buy into it. Instead, go into your imagination and call upon the most wonderful world your imagination can create. Anchor it in your heart with joy and gratitude and then into the Earth. Become a conscious creator of Paradise on Earth.

We have been playing this game for eons of time and the game is now over. We won the game, when collectively on September 11, 2001 and again on December 26, 2004 the critical mass of compassion was reached. Both disasters held the potential to push the collective consciousness further into fear or push us over the top, into compassion. Compassion ruled. Not from our world leaders, but from the common people.

Even before that, participation of thousands of Lightworkers from all over the globe in the Harmonic Convergence in 1987 summoned forth the request for help from our Spiritual Hierarchy and from Source. We prayed for help to create Peace and Love on our planet. We have been receiving this help in the form of higher frequencies of light that are beaming on to the planet.

These light frequencies are raising the frequency of the planet and every body on it. These frequencies are activating the hidden upgraded version of our DNA and expanding our consciousness. For those who, at a soul level, have chosen to stay with Gaia, they must receive and integrate these frequencies and move through the personal transformation that is being activated.

For those who chose not to make this evolutionary leap, they will be leaving the planet and will incarnate in another place, another dimension that will support their soul's growth in a way that is most appropriate to them. There will be a lot of people leaving the planet. Most will leave through the natural means of accidents and disease. Unfortunately some will take their own life as they cannot cope with the high frequencies that make them so uncomfortable.

Mercifully, we won't have as many natural disasters that had been predicted for these end times. Because, for the most part, the Lightworkers of the planet have been doing an excellent job of consciously and unconsciously transmuting the denser energies of fear, anger, hatred, judgment, guilt and shame. This service is making the transformation of the planet progressively more graceful.

The bottom line is: Gaia has chosen to ascend her frequency and consciousness into the fifth dimension. She has chosen to return to Peace and Paradise. She will have her way one way or another. It serves us to "get with her plan" and do it the easier, more graceful way. Anyone who doesn't want to get with that program will have to leave.

In the fifth dimension, the denser energies do not exist. There is instant manifestation. If you make a decision that puts you out of alignment with your Divine Plan, you will get an immediate corrective adjustment. Instant Karma, if you will. You will not be able to store unexpressed thoughts, emotions, imbalances or lessons as holdovers to be dealt with later. Everything is NOW.

The higher light frequencies that are bathing the planet are also flushing up the denser energies. There is a purging of the toxicity (negative emotional energies and experiences). As these are flushed up, they play out one last time on the screen of our reality. Its hidden stuff that has always been there, but we were unwilling to look at. It must be raised up into the light of day if it is to heal.

In addition to the higher frequencies, the Spiritual Hierarchy is also helping you with technical upgrades to your system so that you can effectively operate in Paradise.

The circuitry of your brain and your neurological system is being rewired. Your spiritual body is merging with your physical body. The numerous layers of your light body are being attached to your physical body and you are being made ready for multi-dimensional travel.

Planetary Activation

There was a time in Gaia's past that we could call Paradise. There are numerous stories that explain the fall from fifth dimensional reality to third dimensional reality. Some say it happened by accident. Some say it happened as a result of not going along with God's plan. Some say it was a deliberate altering of our DNA by cosmic genetic scientists wanting to create a slave race. Others say it was simply a natural end of a cycle. We will remember the truth soon enough. However the fall into density happened, it has played out its hand and Gaia and any souls who chose to continue to play with her are on the return to Paradise.

The planetary activation is in full swing. The activations are taking place in 12 waves. The individuals activated in the first wave, like me, are Starseeds from other systems, sent here to move through the transformation first and then assist the others. Our souls have been through this ascension process before. We are experienced teachers and technicians of ascension.

If this book has come into your hands, then you are being activated and ready to integrate the changes and learn how to use the new features of your upgrade. Your number has been called. Your train has pulled into the station. It's up to you. Do you want to take the *Divine Human* train to Paradise?

Immaculate Conception of Paradise

On March 5, 2005 the Paradise Hologram was seeded into the Earth, first through the Hawaiian island of Kaua'i.

In the months leading up to it, I felt that I had been in a strange kind of preparation mode for some really big event that was going to happen. I had the sense that it isn't just me, but the whole planet. Intellectually, I had been aware, and had been telling others that we were anchoring Paradise on Earth. But what does that really mean? How was that going to happen? When would it happen?

Holograms

We live in a holographic reality. Our brains are holographic projectors. They project our conscious and unconscious thoughts and beliefs (film) onto a spherical screen all around us, which we call our reality. Because we are always standing in the middle of the sphere, and because it moves along with us, we believe that this is all there is. We believe that whatever we are seeing on this screen is real because we interact with it and it responds.

Each of us has our own holographic sphere that moves along with our bodies. Sometimes our individual sphere touches the sphere of another and when they touch, the other person becomes real for us. There is a bigger holographic sphere around the Earth that includes us all. What is the hologram made up of? It is a matrix of thoughts and beliefs, dramatized and projected on the screen of our awareness.

So when we share a thought form or belief system, we are included in a holographic sphere with the others that share that belief system. There are many, many holographic spheres, each representing a different belief matrix. These holographic spheres are intersecting and overlaying each other.

Immaculate Conception

When you introduce a new belief matrix into an already existing holographic reality, everything within the holographic reality must morph and change to accommodate the new belief. Rarely is the new belief born clearly and cleanly, without being distorted by the old beliefs.

An immaculate conception occurs when a new hologram can be seeded, nurtured and born without distortion from the existing matrix. The Catholic story of Mary and Jesus is filled with the symbolism that points to this process. Mary, a maiden of unquestionable purity, conceives a child of God, rather than a child of man. Mary, being a representative of the Divine Feminine, has the ability to create a new, clean holographic sphere. The Divine Masculine seeds this sphere with his *Divine Concept* of God in Human form. Mary was able to hold this divine concept within her sphere (womb) while it grew and then she birthed it into the world of form.

Energetically, all the beings of Earth, mostly at an unconscious level, have been going through a purification process. Many of us have been going through this purification process consciously, at an accelerated rate relative to the mass populous. We have become aware of the holographic nature of reality. We have become aware that all reality is illusion. We have become aware that we can change our experience of reality by changing our belief structure. We have found ways to consciously change our belief matrix and found our personal holographic realities changing in response.

Mother Earth herself has been clearing the old belief matrices she has been holding. She has been going through a purification process. Her sphere (holographic screen) is being cleaned and cleared because She has decided to host a new holographic reality.

We have consciously chosen to assist in the transformation from one reality to a new one. We have consciously chosen to serve as midwives for the Divine Concept of Paradise on Earth. And some of us have committed to allowing the Paradise Hologram to move through our bodies and energy fields so that we become human expressions of Paradise.

Paradise

Who are we and why are we here? Every indigenous people and every religion has a creation story. This creation story itself is a belief matrix, comprised of many assumptions that form the basis, the structure of the shared holographic reality on a planet. Looking at the various creation stories on Earth, you will find that they all have a similar plot.

We started out in something called Paradise, then something happened that led to some kind of "fall" or falling out with the Creator. Then suffering and strife began a downward spiral that has taken us to the brink of self-destruction. Within the creation stories seems to be the potential for a return to Paradise if we play our cards right.

What if we were to be suddenly faced with proof of a different creation story? The whole structure of our belief matrix would change, along with it — our shared holographic reality.

Everyone's idea of Paradise will be a little bit different. As creator of your own reality, you will create your own version. Here are some of the main characteristics that I have foreseen.

- A global temperate climate
- Abundant supply of everything we desire
- Whatever you desire is already yours for the claiming
- Perfect health
- Immortality
- A playful, celebratory approach to everyday life
- Living your passion
- Giving your unique gifts freely in joyful service, on your terms
- Receiving the unique gifts of others freely in their joyful service to you
- Peace and harmony
- Unity in diversity
- Respect for all consciousness
- Instant manifestation of your desires
- Instant dematerialization of that which is no longer desired
- Free flow of all types of energy
- Teleportation
- Telepathic communication
- Personal sovereignty
- Full consciousness
- Stewardship of the planet

- Harmonious membership in Galactic Federation of Light

Kaua'i

The island of Kaua'i is a special place on Earth, most closely resonating with the Paradise frequency. It is said to be the original birthplace, the port of entry into the Earth realm of Starseeds from many other dimensional realities. I personally know many people who have moved here to Kaua'i within the last few years, feeling called back "home" to hold the immaculate concept of Paradise until it is ready to be born on this Earth. Whether they were aware of the conception event on 03/05/2005 or not, their presence here was facilitating, supporting and nurturing this Immaculate Conception.

From Kaua'i, this Paradise Hologram will spread out and infuse itself into the core of Mother Earth and then outward to fill the atmosphere around it. At the physical level, there might not be an immediate notice of it. For those who are super sensitive to subtle energy, they might notice something different. Just like a woman who may just "know" that she has just conceived. Most women are not aware of this at all.

So we have conception, gestation and then birth. I believe that when the birth takes place we will see more evidence of the change reflected back to us on the screen of our holographic reality. My guess is that soon, the mass populace will be confronted with evidence of a new creation story — a new and expanded version of who we are and why we are here. That new creation story will trigger massive changes in our physical reality that will begin to align with the Paradise Hologram that was conceived on March 5.

Anatomy of a Divine Human

What is a *Divine Human* and why would you want to be one? What are the practical advantages? Isn't divinity just for avatars like Buddha, Jesus and Mohamed? And if you decide it would be a good idea, how do you transform from "only human" to "*Divine Human?*"

By definition every human is Divine. The human being is the *Sacred Union* of the individualized consciousness of All That Is and physical matter. Humans are the *Sacred Union* of Spirit and Earth. Yet people are aware of their own Divine nature in varying degrees. People express their divinity in varying degrees.

As our individual consciousness journeyed into the density of matter, we have felt disconnected from our spiritual source. We have fallen asleep and dreamt that we are separate from our own Divinity. The process used in the *Divine Human Upgrades* is a spiritual technology that helps us to awaken and clear away the dream of separation. We rebirth ourselves into the world of form with the awakened knowing that we are *Divine Humans* creating Paradise on Earth.

Practically speaking — what's in it for you? Why would you focus any attention, time, energy or resources into such a transformation? For many people, spiritual growth is something that waits on the back burner until all the practical issues of survival, safety, emotional connections and self-esteem are comfortably mastered.

Male/Female Integration

Energy has patterns of movement and we can call one pattern male, the other female. The male pattern of movement is assertive; it initiates action. Look at the male genitalia as an example. It is outside the body, action oriented. It takes pleasure in moving against the walls of an enclosure. In humans it expresses itself through the mind. It seeks to organize, analyze, understand, and find the limits. Male energy expresses itself through the mind, seeking to master the physical world. All human beings have a male aspect to themselves, sometimes called the inner male.

Likewise, each individual has an inner female. This energy pattern is receptive and responsive — an open space with defined boundaries. The open space is dark and mysterious. It seems empty, but is pregnant with the possibility of anything and everything. The feminine is comfortable with the unknown. From this mystery springs creativity and intuition. It is the womb — nourishing and nurturing. Female energy expresses through the heart, through the senses — using its creativity to give birth to an outer space that is inviting, nourishing and sensual.

Ideally, each individual would have healthy, mature male and female aspects working together as equal partners. Yet, this is rarely the case. As humans experience the slings and arrows of life, their inner males and/or females become wounded, and their development arrested.

The inner male and inner female of a *Divine Human* are completely healed, whole, balanced and harmoniously playing in *Sacred Union* within.

Sacred Union Consciousness is the integration of male and female energies at all levels of your being. To upgrade yourself into a *Divine Human*, you start with male/female integration at the personality level and you end with male/female integration at the Divine-Spark level.

Emotional Body

A *Divine Human*'s emotional body is clear. There are no suppressed or unexpressed emotions. The reason we encounter hurtful situations is because of the hurtful energy that is stored inside our emotional body. The soul is always seeking to bring us back to health and joy. It is trying to release the hidden and suppressed energy. It uses the law of attraction (like attracts like) to magnetize the people and situations to us that will trigger the opportunity for release.

For example, if you have suppressed anger, your soul will decide that it is unhealthy and will create a drama where somebody else who has anger issues will trigger your anger. The soul's purpose for doing this is so that you will release the anger inside of you by expressing it.

Yet most of us have been trained **not** to express our anger. It isn't nice. We suppress it again or we express it in passive aggressive ways. If we don't express it somehow, it will eventually lead to disease within the body. Or we could erupt in a rage, releasing pent up anger disproportionate to the current situation.

If we clear the emotional body in an alternative, graceful way, our soul won't have to create those hurtful dramas anymore. Then our spirit is free to create magical, mystical adventures that reflect the clarity of our emotional body.

Now that doesn't mean that as a *Divine Human,* you won't don't experience pain from time to time. That's the human part. Although I must admit, the frequency goes down. The difference is that the emotional pain will move through you like a wave. Express it honestly in the moment, with respect and compassion and then let it go. It won't be stored in your emotional body.

Do you realize how much energy it takes to hold on to emotional pain? You spend an enormous amount of energy defending it, lest it trigger a tidal wave. When the emotional body is cleansed, all of that defensive energy is freed up to be used to restore health and express yourself creatively.

Mental Body

It is important to understand the difference between the mind, the brain and their relationship to the body. The **brain** is a biocomputer similar to the CPU (central processing unit) in your personal computer. The brain is hardwired to operate the body. All the instructions for running the body are in the brain. The central nervous system is the communication network that delivers instructions from the brain to all the other parts of the body. The brain uses Creative Source Energy from your Divine Spark as its power source.

The **mind** is not localized in the brain. It lives in an energetic field in and around your physical body called a mental body. The mind is a software program installed around the body to create and maintain the illusion of duality/polarity on this planet. It is like putting on a game helmet to play a virtual reality game at the arcade.

The body does not need the mind, at all, to function. It just needs the brain. As a matter of fact, this mental energetic field lies in between Creative Source Energy and the brain and creates the Illusion of Separation from Source.

The mind is an artificial intelligence software program. Computer scientists have created artificial intelligence software that simulates the mind. We use the term "intelligence" because the software starts with a specific set of programs and then self-generates new programs as it "learns." Learning is different from knowing. When you draw on Divine Intelligence you "know" the truth. There is no learning involved.

The mind "learns" by observing patterns and cause-effect relationships. When it observes a similar pattern several times, it creates a rule. Then it stores the data relative to that new rule. The rule then becomes a subprogram of the mind. We call these subprograms beliefs and treat them as if they are truth. These beliefs are just a collection of observed cause-effect relationships, with associated stories that create anecdotal validation that the rule is true.

The mind also acts as a filter. There is so much happening in creation and the mind filters out most of it. It does this to help you focus your attention on this physical reality. The input devices for our software program called the mind are our senses: sight, sound, smell, taste and touch. These are the only input devices that the mind values. Yes, we do receive A LOT of information in other ways. We call this intuition. Yet the mind does not value information received intuitively and will more often than not cast doubt upon it. However, many of us have trained ourselves to value this other kind of intuitive input, suggesting that there is another awareness within us that is not the mind.

Creative Source Energy must pass through this mental software program on the way to the brain. Creative Source Energy doesn't make any judgments about the usefulness of these software programs. Remember the analogy of the movie projector? In a similar way, your Creative Source Energy (light source) flows through your mind, shining through your DNA (film) and the brain (movie projector) projects a holographic image that you perceive as reality. Your body is a hologram. Everything in physical form is a hologram.

Disney and other studios are already producing holographic images using crystal lasers. The holographic images projected by the brain are denser than the holographic images projected by Disney, so we perceive the brain-generated holograms as more "real."

What is DNA then? It is information, records — data. The DNA contains the blueprint for your physical body. It stores information about all of your life experiences including emotions, thoughts and thought patterns, judgments, belief systems and your self-image. It includes records about your experiences as other aspects of yourself in other dimensional reality (past or alternate lives). Your DNA contains the records for your life's purpose. It contains the blueprint for your Divine Body, which is what we are evolving into as a species. Your DNA includes the data recorded and stored by your mind, but is much more.

The mind is also programmed to create a self-image and is doing so during the first seven years of your life. As your mind creates your self image by observing the cause and effect relationships that are your early experiences. These observations are based on the limited input of your senses and your incomplete and immature perception as your mind assigns meaning to what you observe. Once the self-image is constructed, the mind job is to protect that self image. It does this by blocking further "learning" that might change it. Again, the Creative Source Energy moves through the software subprogram called "self" and projects holographic movies that reflect that self-image.

Whenever we attempt to expand, improve or change that self-image, the mind goes into protection mode and will conjure up a drama that will seem to validate that original self-image subprogram.

A *Divine Human*, recognizing that the mind is an artificial intelligence software program, upgrades the software so that it will embrace the true Divine self image. It purges the subprograms (subconscious) that do not support the true Divine self image. A *Divine Human* has no subconscious, deep conscious or connection to mass unconscious. A *Divine Human* is a fully conscious and aware being. A *Divine Human* brings its own Divine Plan into the solar plexus and connects directly to the God/Goddess mind.

As information is needed, it flows into the God/Goddess consciousness in NOW moment to maintain alignment with its own Divine Plan. A *Divine Human* stays in impeccable integrity by honoring its own Divine Plan (Divine Will) in every moment and allows all others to honor whatever they feel is in their highest good. Judgment is replaced by discernment of your personal alignment with your Divine Will. Non-judgment + allowance = compassion.

Spiritual Body

My definition for spiritual body is the circulatory system for energy in and around the body. This would include the prana tube, chakra systems and the meridian pathways that move energy and consciousness through the physical, emotional and mental bodies. The chakras are multi dimensional connections to other aspects of yourself in other times and other dimensions. Consciousness from what you might call past or parallel lives flow to you through the chakra portals. You are also connected to your soul family through the chakra portals. Other people, who have emotional attachments to you, or you to them, connect in your chakras.

Your energy body is connected to an energy grid of mass consciousness. There is more than one mass consciousness grid around this planet. The one you connect to will be determined by the frequency that your holographic biocomputer (body) transmits. Like attracts like. More on this in a moment.

A *Divine Human*'s spiritual body is clear. Lessons, issues, karma, vows, agreements and contracts from parallel lives are brought forward into consciousness, healed, balanced and released. This represents total freedom at all levels of your being.

Physical Body

Clearing the emotional, mental and spiritual body of disharmony allows the physical body to restore itself to balance, harmony and optimum health. All disease starts in these three outer bodies and if they remain in your energy field (aura) for long enough, they will move into the physical body, creating blockages to the flow of Creative Source Energy. Wherever Creative Source Energy does not flow, dis-ease can manifest.

It is hard to predict how long it might take the physical body to return to radiant health. Of course much is dependent on how much organic damage has already been caused. I have found in my healing facilitation practice that when the emotional, mental and spiritual core issues are released, often a client will suddenly become aware of new medical (allopathic or holistic) technologies that leads them to eventual restoration of heath. It seems that as long as their issues go unreleased, the mind will filter out awareness of the solution. I have also seen many immediate physical healings. Healing miracles are on the rise and present everywhere.

New healing technologies will continue to be brought through as more people embrace their Divine Intelligence and remember how to restore the body to balance and harmony.

Frequency

Frequency is a measurement of the speed at which energy moves. Everything is energy. Love is the only energy there is. Compassion is the highest frequency of love and fear is the lowest frequency of love. Many teachers say that fear is the opposite of love. But there can be no opposite to All That Is. Some teachers say that fear and love cannot exist in the same place. I agree. Not because they are opposites, but because of the Law of Harmonics.

The Law of Harmonics, which is a universal law, states that energies that are of differing frequencies must harmonize. That is why you might be in a good mood, come into the presence of a friend who is in bad mood and then walk away feeling not so good as before. Your frequency decreases and your friend's raises and your frequencies harmonize in the middle. There is a certain point in your evolving Divinity where your high frequency cannot decrease. At that point, the presence of lower frequencies will not affect you. Others who come in contact with you will automatically be lifted to harmonize with you — at least for a while. That is why it feels so good to be in the presence of a *Divine*

Human. You will find people want to hang around you and get high on your aura.

Divine Humans are masters of frequency. They can call upon whatever frequency they like and can transmute a situation immediately. Fear transmutes (raises its frequency) in the presence of higher frequencies of love (compassion).

Each human emotion has a specific frequency. And frequencies are often associated with color. People may describe feeling "blue" which we understand as sad or melancholy. Someone might describe feeling "green with envy." Joy is often associated with the color yellow, and so on.

On the visible light spectrum, orange is a higher frequency than red. Yellow is a higher frequency than orange, followed by green, blue, violet and the highest frequency is white. Many *Divine Humans* will represent themselves or their work using a rainbow image, acknowledging their mastery of frequency. Each frequency (all are aspects of love) has a different specialty or purpose.

I like to use a frequency called Passionate Compassion for transmutation, which is a red-violet color. This frequency is a synergistic blend of the Violet Ray of Transmutation, the Pink Ray of Compassion and the Red Ray of Passion.

Using guided imagery, which directs the energy, I will guide a client to breathe a denser emotional energy, say anger, into an imaginary sphere that will fill up like a balloon. Once all the anger is blown into the sphere, we call in the ray of Passionate Compassion (red-violet beam of light from Source) into the container. The Law of Harmonics gets busy raising the frequency of the anger to match the higher frequency of Passionate Compassion. Before you know it, the container is filled with a beautiful red-violet energy which the client then brings back into the emotional body. In effect, we love the anger into a higher frequency. This is a graceful way to affect transformation. There is no judgment, no denial and no banishment of less desirable "stuff." There is the very clear acknowledgement that "all there is — is love" waiting to ascend to a higher frequency or state of being.

Our bodies are energy receivers and transmitters very much like a radio. We can "tune-in" to different frequencies associated with states of consciousness like selecting stations on the radio. Just like on a radio, there are a variety of stations: country-western, oldies, easy-listening, classical, top-ten music hits, talk radio, news radio, etc. Each station has its own feel, flavor, focus — consciousness. Each station has a band width of frequency associated with it. You might be able to tune into the oldie station by placing dial somewhere between 79.9 and 81.2. There is a point where the reception is the clearest, yet there is some reception a few degrees in either direction.

Dimensions of Consciousness

Likewise, there is a bandwidth of frequency related to dimensions of consciousness. We have probably heard about third, fourth and fifth dimensional consciousness. Each dimension of consciousness, just like a radio station, has its own characteristics, flavor, structure and rules. The main difference between them, as far as I can tell, is density and flexibility or ease of movement from one state of being to another.

The third dimension is the densest. Change does not happen very easily or quickly. Structures and rules seem rigid and severely enforced. Everything seems more solid and dense including physical objects, ideas and thought constructs such as time and space.

The fourth dimension is less dense than the third, and a bit more fluid. Time and space seem more flexible and I have fun experimenting with expanding and contracting time and space to meet my needs. Most people on this planet are vibrating at a frequency in the bandwidth of the fourth dimension. They may not notice a big difference from the third because the habitual thought patterns hold energy in form. But when people begin opening to new thoughts, letting go of habitual movement, they find that life changes a lot more easily and quickly in response.

The fifth dimension — songs were written about it and we imagined that utopia lived in the fifth dimension. Yet it is here, already anchored on this planet. Many Lightworkers are operating in the fifth dimension. Indeed, it is much less dense than the third or fourth. Life seems more mystical and magical. Synchronicity runs high. Spontaneous healings occur. Manifesting seems easier.

People tuned into this frequency experience more joy, love, bliss and are more centered, clear and open-hearted. They have probably consciously worked at clearing much of their past and attempt to live in the NOW moment as frequently as they can.

The sixth and seventh dimensions have been anchored onto the planet, which means we can raise our frequency to tune into these dimensions. The sixth vibrates at a frequency above the soul-level connections and contracts. It vibrates at a level above the electromagnetic polarity grid. My frequency is now tuned into the sixth dimension and life here is much quieter, more peaceful. I am not connected to the mass consciousness polarity grid. No more fear; more joy, more bliss. The pleasure receptors of my body are much more sensitive. Yahoo!!! Lovemaking takes on a whole new meaning when you experience full body orgasms with just a kiss. Of course, Casey's electric kundalini transmissions have a lot to do with it. This is another benefit of *Sacred Union Partnership* that I love.

Manifestation is even faster here. My consciousness opened up and new understandings are being downloaded. The dynamics of our illusionary reality are revealing themselves to me. It's all illusion. When you understand how the illusion is constructed, you can master it. I am finally able to finish this book. It is flowing easily and effortlessly; a life-long dream finally realized. I have programmed my holographic biocomputer to drop everything below the sixth dimension, so there is some fluctuation within the bandwidth, but I'm no longer dipping down below it.

I'm aware of the chaos of the world, but it cannot touch me. I feel safe. There is no guilt about leaving the lower dimensional realities behind. Think of it this way. When you get on a plane and the flight attendant gives the safety talk, you are told that in case of emergency, put the oxygen mask on yourself first and then assist others. My oxygen mask is on and I can more effectively help others by exploring the higher dimensions and then reporting back and teaching others how to get here too. It doesn't do me or anyone else any good to run around trying to save others and suffocating myself in the process. My savior complex has been released and integrated. As long as my body is on the planet, then I am serving as an acupuncture needle to ground higher frequencies — still doing my part by just walking around.

The seventh dimension vibrates at the Shambhalla and Shangri-La frequency (Seventh Heaven) where the Ascended Masters hang out. I'm not there yet, but Spirit tells me I can enter into the seventh dimension by July. I'm told it's another whole dynamic and that is the dimension where you can connect with your Twin Ray. Many Ascended Masters are looking forward to Twin Ray Completion. I'll let you know when I get there.

Mass Consciousness Grids

At this time there are at least three mass consciousness grids around the planet. The one most people are connected to is the polarity grid that runs on the surface of the Earth. Just like our minds are an auxiliary artificial intelligence software program for our bodies, Mother Earth, has one for her body as well. It has all the polarity programs loaded into it. It is what is described in the movie Matrix. Right now the grid is being heavily bombarded by fear-based propaganda and it is affecting the emotional body of everyone plugged into it. When you are plugged into this grid, you can tune into the third, fourth, and up to mid-level fifth dimensions.

Another grid is called the God/Goddess Grid, or the Shambhalla/Shangri-La Grid. This begins at the mid-fifth dimension and will expand, with no limits, to include higher and higher dimensions as they are anchored onto the planet. We can disconnect our bodies from the polarity grid and connect with the God/Goddess Grid. But to do so we must release all density and raise our frequency to at least the upper fifth dimension.

A ninth dimensional grid of pure compassion is currently intact around the outside of the planet. Remembering the Law of Harmonics, eventually the whole Earth will raise her frequency to match this grid.

The Upgrades

I've explained the *Anatomy of a Divine Human*, using the computer as a metaphor. The body is a holographic biocomputer with mind software. The computer and its software can be upgraded to host our *Sacred Union* Consciousness.

Let's take this metaphor a little further. Those of us, who are not computer programmers, don't spend much time thinking about the next software upgrade that *MicroSoft* or *Apple* may come up with. We use what we have as tools to get our tasks done. There are computer programmers who love to express themselves creatively by dreaming up new tools, programs and upgrades. It's their passion and a great creative outlet for their knowledge, gifts and talents. When they unveil a new product, we evaluate it to see if it has value in our lives, and choose to buy it or not.

Every once in a while an upgrade comes along that is such a big change, a whole new operating system is needed to support all the wonderful new features and abilities. Everybody wants to get it and it seems that if you don't jump on the bandwagon, you are left far behind.

We are evolving quickly, into a new life-form. It is an evolution of consciousness to be sure, yet there are certain technical aspects related to the four-body system that must be upgraded to host the expanding consciousness. If it is your Divine Plan to make this evolutionary step in this lifetime, you are probably going through some of these upgrades already without being conscious of it.

As each of the 12 upgrade waves is activated, it serves the human hosts to align with the upgrade, integrate it as gracefully as possible and begin using the new features the upgrades allow.

I call myself a Spiritual Midwife, birthing the *Divine Human* into *Sacred Union Consciousness*. At the same time, I see myself as a passionate holographic computer designer and technician. I love discovering the dynamics of how we construct our illusionary realities. I love creatively expressing my discoveries, through guided visualizations. I have a passion for creating new playgrounds and then inviting you, my Divine Playmates, to come play with me.

I have identified the following upgrades which softly, gracefully and lovingly help you install the new system upgrades. As a *Divine Human*, I command and create the reality that just by your command (if it is in alignment with your own Divine Plan) you will receive the upgrades. Each upgrade will install itself at an appropriate time for you, giving you the time and space you need to integrate the changes comfortably, easily and gracefully before you install the next.

New Operating System

Our disks are being formatted. All of us are being outfitted with a New Operating System that will change our parameters. When a computer gets a new operating system, it changes many of the Old Settings, even if we liked them. It gives the computer a whole new face. It opens up new possibilities for sure.

This is what is happening to all of us. We are star trekking. We are going where no (hu)man has gone before; not in this way, in the manner where all levels, galactic, solar and universe are so affected. All planets will be affected by our new operating systems. We are being given an opportunity to not hold on to what we think we are: quite possibly we are more than that. We are given a chance to see learn that we do NOT see things as they are; we see them as We Are!

Our TOOLS are changing, our WINDOWS are opening, and HELP is on the way. The celestial kingdoms are inserting more light into us and we are being EDITED in ways that we cannot yet comprehend. We are being RE-FORMATTED for a higher consciousness. We have to stay OPEN, we can't be closed. Our PROPERTIES are changing. We might have to FIND some new things and REPLACE some old things. We may benefit by UNDOing certain behaviors that we have followed for a long time. We are CLEARing out our lower levels. We are DELETING Separation. EXTRACTING Polarity. ERASING Duality. UNDOing Linear Time. We will GO TO a higher station. We need to re-think what has been NORMAL. We are coming back ON LINE as citizens of the Universe. Our old RULERS and measurements no longer work. We are DOCUMENTING ourselves as MASTERS. ZOOMing in on Higher Truths. BREAKing with the past. CROSS-REFERENCING our lineages and heritages. Opening up our FIELDS and finding new SYMBOLS. We are HYPER-LINKING with our Multidimensionality. Creating new TEMPLATES AND PLUG-INS. Changing our STYLES. Letting go of our BACKGROUNDS.

After all, we are DOWNLOADING The Higher Blueprint of the Perfected Species for Humanity. Co-creating Heaven on Earth. We are Re-solving the Missed Story. Re-solving Separation. We are Moving into a Room with a More Expansive View. We are receiving a New Operating System appropriate for New Earth. Isn't this amazing?

Wistancia Stone, www.wistancia.com

That's what I'm talking about. The *Divine Human Upgra*des are DEFRAG for the soul.

The next seven chapters describe the seven upgrades.

1. *Sacred Union* of the Inner Male and Female
2. Clearing the Pain Body
3. Out'ta Your Mind
4. Embracing Abundance
5. Integrating Polarity
6. The Divine Birth
7. Twin Flame Completion

Within each chapter, I will give you:

- A description of the upgrade
- The upgrade installation command
- Integration instructions and examples
- New feature benefits and practice exercises

These upgrades move you into conscious *Sacred Union* with your own Divinity. Oddly enough, these upgrades match closely with ascension teachings of the ancient mystery schools. In those days, the upgrades were called initiations.

The Mystery Schools contained bodies of knowledge and ascension technology that was only available to the royalty of the day. Priests and priestesses served in the temples, exacting harsh discipline from the initiates.

Many of the initiations themselves are so demanding that failure to move through them correctly would result in your death. Some souls have been reincarnated numerous times, to live through the initiation and move on to the next.

Initiation, as the word implies, is just the beginning. You must then move through practice and mastery.

So we are in a new time. We are in a new place in the evolution of our planet. No longer will we keep the sacred teachings a mystery to all but the elite. They are for all who want to partake. No longer do they take grueling discipline. Although a little bit of effort is required to learn the new features. Practice using them until you master them and they become natural.

A note about the installation command statements that are included in each chapter. They are similar to an AUTOEXEC file for computer software. They automatically install the upgrade. Use it, if, and only if, you want to activate the upgrade. They are not to be taken lightly for they will launch you into deep transformation, at the level of your DNA. How do you know if they work? You will start changing. Your life will start changing. It is possible that some of these changes have already begun. In which case, this book gives you a better understanding of what is happening within you.

If you choose to activate the upgrades, please do so **one at a time**. Give yourself at least a week in between the initiations, so that you may integrate the changes gracefully. The *Journey to Sacred Union* is one of self love. Love yourself enough to go slow and easy with these changes.

There may be a significant variance between your current life and living in alignment with your Divine Plan. Allow the transition to be graceful. Flow with the changes as they arise. Know whatever you need to let go of from your former life, will be replaced by something much lighter, more beautiful and more aligned with "Who You Really Are" — a *Divine Human* co-creating and enjoying Paradise on Earth.

These upgrades are also delivered via live via teleclasses and recorded on CDs. There are advantages to each delivery system.

The most supportive, self-loving way to receive these upgrades is to participate in a teleclass and use the 10-CD kit to help align the subconscious with the upgrades during dreamtime. Of course, this is also the most expensive because it includes the time and energy of an upgrade facilitator for the teleclasses. It also gives you the benefit of the group energy to lean on, which makes integration much more graceful.

The next most supportive option is to use the Self-Study CD kit to move through the upgrades on your own. In this, you have the advantage of relaxing into a meditative state, being guided through the beautiful inner journey recorded for each upgrade. My love for initiation and sacred ceremony, along with the words and images that the DNA understands, creates a wonderful experience that you will be free to listen to as often as you like. Here you have the advantage of moving through the initiations at your own pace.

If you are contemplating this option, please be honest with yourself. Are you the type of person who has enough self-discipline to move through this on your own? Many people purchase the kit, and then let all kinds of other life demands distract them from completing (and even beginning) the upgrades.

For many people, the teleclasses provide that appointment time that they will set aside and honor because they know they are part of a group. There is no judgment about self-discipline needed here. I ask you to lovingly acknowledge and accept how you operate most effectively.

The third option is to only use the book and the installation commands. This will work, but you will miss out on the beauty of the upgrade inner journey as presented by the creative visualization in the Teleclasses and CDs.

I Am The Holy Grail

Upgrade Description

In this upgrade, we call to the surface all hidden and suppressed energies of separation, abandonment, betrayal, rejection, victimhood, pain, sorrow and grief for release and transmutation.

We give the command to release blame (forgive) perceptions of separation from male relationships; including the male aspect of your concept of God, physical fathers, brothers, sons, husbands, lovers, your own male aspect and any other man you have ever known. In the same way, we command the release of perceptions of separation from all the related female relationships. We are clearing from this lifetime as well as from all other aspects of ourselves that are experiencing life in any other time or dimension.

After clearing the perceptions and dense energies from the four-body system, we turn our attention to your own inner male, inner female and inner child. We take a look at what condition they are in. We shine the light of Passionate Compassion upon them so that they will heal and mature into radiantly healthy, well-balanced beings that will work together in *Sacred Union* within you.

Then we bring in the Clear Crystal Patterns of the male aspect of your Oversoul Matrix. We bring in the Sapphire Blue Crystal Patterns of the female aspect of your Oversoul Matrix.

The Oversoul Matrix is that aspect of you that operates above polarity. It is the consciousness that remembers and has directed all of your incarnations. It does not see your actions as good or evil. It sees through the eyes of soul growth through experience. It sets up opportunities for soul growth by attracting dramas to you for your experience. It is the place where your soul and spirit merge. It is the next higher level of consciousness. At this level of consciousness, you feel the oneness of Who You Really Are. You feel the oneness of All That Is. At the same time, you know yourself as an individual expression of All That Is. You access both the oneness and the individuality.

In this upgrade, after you have cleared the density of past wounding in all of your relationships, you become like the purified bride; ready to receive the bridegroom. So you marry the male/female Oversoul Matrix in *Sacred Union*, merging inside your body. The inner child also merges with them, transmuting into the Divine Child.

Installation Command

I AM That I AM. I AM That I AM. I AM That I AM. I now command the activation of the *Divine Human Upgrade* called *Sacred Union of the Male and Female*. I open my heart and command all levels of my consciousness to fully to receive the gifts of this upgrade. I command my outer self to allow and embrace the needed lessons and changes this upgrade brings into my life now. I command easy, comfortable, graceful and joyful integration of the new features, higher frequencies and expanded consciousness delivered through this upgrade. So Be It. So It Is.

Integration

As you let go of the hidden and suppressed slings and arrows of the past and replace that cellular memory with the higher frequencies of light — you raise your frequency. And as your frequency continues to ascend to higher and higher levels — your Divinity descends to meet it and takes up residence in your physical body. You are anchoring your Divinity onto the Earth, blessed one. In so doing, you are doing your part to anchor Paradise on Earth.

As you move through this transition, you may experience some discomforts that are usually associated with what we might call growing pains. These discomforts arise because you have raised your frequency and your awareness. But you may still be living in the middle of the forms that you created in an earlier level of frequency and awareness. The forms I am speaking of are things like relationships, jobs, physical locations, life styles, habits and behavior patterns. Do not be attached to the forms. They are temporary and they will shift now to align with your new level of frequency and consciousness.

Relationships might shift or dissolve. You might find that you are uncomfortable in your home or location. Your job might become too uncomfortable to bear. Let go of these forms — or you might find that the universe just moves them away from you.

Practice Exercises

When you experience an upgrade initiation, you are walking through a new doorway. What lies beyond the doorway is all new and it takes some adjustment time. The transformation process is one of initiation, practice and then mastery. Initiation happens in a moment of time, for example during a teleclass or CD session. After that, there is no way to predict how long you will need to practice to reach mastery of a new way of being.

You will create practice exercises for yourself. I don't like to call them tests. The word "test," for most of us, comes with an ominous feeling that if we don't pass it, we have somehow failed. This is not the case when you are practicing to reach mastery.

In this world of form, we gain mastery by creating mini-dramas in our life. The mini-dramas you create when you are practicing mastery will relate to walking through a situation that, in the past, might have triggered a patterned response. You may create scenarios where common triggers are introduced. Then you have an opportunity to move through the mini-drama in a new way. You will know you have reached mastery when that trigger no longer presents itself.

Let's look at an example. In this first initiation, *Sacred Union of the Inner Male/Female*; we are releasing patterns of separation, abandonment, betrayal, rejection and victimhood. Remember, the Law of Attraction, like attracts like. Everybody you are in relationship with (any type), has been attracted to you based on the frequency you transmit and the issues you want to heal. We draw people into our lives, as mirrors, to reflect back to us what we need to heal. At a subconscious level, we contract with them to create an environment where mutual healing and integration is a potential. We constantly seek to know and love ourselves at deeper and deeper levels.

When you go through a *Divine Human Upgrade*, your frequency raises quite drastically. You also heal issues and complete contracts at many levels. After an upgrade, all your relationships are subject to change or dissolution.

Imagine that you have a partner in your life and your contract with each other is to heal a pattern of abandonment. Of course, this is a subconscious agreement. If it were conscious, you probably wouldn't enter into the relationship at all. A typical abandonment pattern would be, at first you resist opening your heart at all. Then you finally trust enough to let your heart open and connect with the other person. Then you enjoy the connection for a while. Just when you are beginning to relax into the relationship, a situation presents itself that creates an end to the relationship. Since most of us don't believe in happy endings, also inherent in the situation is a "good reason" for the relationship to end.

Let's look at this again from a Conscious Creator point-of-view. Again, your contract with your partner is to heal a pattern of abandonment. One or both of you decide to participate in a *Divine Human Upgrade* session and release abandonment issues in this alternate, more graceful way. So your contract with your partner comes to completion. If that is the only reason you are together, then the change in frequency will probably make being with this partner uncomfortable.

This time around, you honestly express what you are feeling, such as, "I feel complete with this relationship and very grateful that you have supported me in letting go of my fear of abandonment." At this point, depending on whether your partner feels complete or healed, there will be loving agreement or a drama that, in your partner's mind, makes for a good reason for separating. The difference for you, this time, is that a change in the form of your relationship doesn't feel like abandonment. You can let go of the form of the relationship and still continue to love, respect and wish the best for your partner. You don't go into judgment or blame for yourself or your partner or try to analyze what went wrong. Nothing went wrong. There is no failure. There is only gratitude and completion of a major life issue.

On the other hand, you may find that once you let go of your abandonment issues, your relationship improves. It could be that because of your fear of abandonment, you were creating distance and defenses. When you let go of your defense strategies, you become more vulnerable and more approachable – more able to perceive and receive the love that was there all the time. You may find that what you perceived as rejection was nothing more than your own projected expectations of eventual abandonment.

When you change your frequency and gracefully heal yourself, many people in your life may feel a difference at a subconscious level. They will feel "not connected" to you anymore. Whenever we still have unexpressed thoughts or emotions with people, there is an energy connection where energy may be drained from you. When you break these inappropriate energy connections, they can feel it. They might call you up out of the blue and try to re-establish a connection.

One of my clients reported to me that after doing the first *Divine Human Upgrade*, all of the men she had dated in the past several years called her up and asked her for a date. What was that about? They were probably feeding off her energy field all this time. When she disconnected, by calling back her energy, they suddenly felt the need to re-establish the connection. She called on her own inner guidance to discern whether to meet with them or not. In all cases, after spending just a little time with each one, she knew that she had brought her contracts with these men to completion and was free to let them go.

Another client told me that his brother suddenly starting picking fights with him after the first *Divine Human Upgrade*. What was happening? The brother felt a change in my client's energy, but couldn't quite understand what that meant — just that he wasn't comfortable with the change. The brother picked fights to create a good reason not to spend time with my client anymore. My client understood what was really happening and just let the relationship go without making the brother wrong or taking his behavior personally. He allowed his brother to have his own level of consciousness without needing to change it or fight to make himself right.

When you are releasing anger, you might create a practice exercise that normally would trigger your anger. We usually feel angry when our boundaries have been violated, or integrity is breeched or when we give away our power. The practice in this case is to be conscious of why you feel triggered, express it with respect and compassion, and then let go of the outcome. If you need help learning how to express yourself with respect and compassion in the face of anger and rage, look into *Nonviolent Communication* seminars, developed by Marshall B. Rosenberg, PhD. He has trained facilitators all over the world and has helped save many relationships.

If you are clearing victimhood issues, you might suddenly become very aware of all of the ways you have been feeling like a victim in your life. Or you might be accused by someone else of making them into a victim. Victim thoughts and feelings come up to the surface for release. Just acknowledge them and let them go.

Grief is a common feeling after upgrades. It is hard to believe, but we actually miss our mind-created identity even if it has caused us lots of pain and suffering. It seems like an old familiar friend has died. Allow yourself expression of grief and all other thoughts and emotions that show up.

Expressing yourself moves the thoughts and emotions out of your system. Find safe ways to express yourself. Don't feel that you have to verbalize your thoughts and feelings to all people in your life. Be discerning. Most people won't be able to handle the intense thoughts and feelings that you have been suppressing for years. Remember, you have drawn these people into your life, subconsciously contracting with them to facilitate your healing. You may have asked them to trigger you, but they probably weren't the ones to wound you in the first place. Most of the original wounding took place many lifetimes ago.

The idea is to MOVE the energy by expression. Try writing, running, drumming, any physical exercise, talking into a tape recorder, drawing, dancing. What ever works! The first step is releasing suppressed thoughts and emotions from the past. When that process is complete, then stay in integrity with yourself and others by continuously communicating the truth from your heart with respect and compassion.

If you need coaching during your integration period, please contact us at Reality Crafting. Either I or one of my trained facilitators will set up a coaching program to help you through the transformation with grace.

The Void

You may enter a period of time known as the void. The void is a wonderful time. It is the space of creation. It is the time in between. It is as if you are sitting down to dinner and you have finished eating the first course and the plates have been cleared away. You are now waiting for the next course to be served. The next course will be served. This is also a time of great trust. It is an opportunity to exercise patience, a trust that everything will manifest in Divine Right Timing. You have heard it said that the universe loves and lives to fill a void. The void is necessary. It is good. It is confirmation that you have successfully let go of the past. Now you have created space for the new forms.

You may experience the void at any or all of the four levels — emotionally, mentally, physically and spiritually.

You may experience an emotional void as feeling empty or not getting emotionally charged anymore. If you were used to riding an emotional roller coaster, you will notice a difference here. If you were very attracted to drama, you may even find this disappointing, or at least, non-stimulating. You will find that situations that used to push your buttons — don't any more. This is actually a lack of attachment. You may drop your attachments to a person, to a situation, to an activity. You may experience a lack of attachment to particular outcomes. This non-attachment to outcomes is very desirable. It does not suggest a lack of caring — but a sense of loving allowance for things to be as they are. And a loving allowance for others to be where they are. For you begin to realize that in every moment, everything and everyone are just as they should be. It is all good. It is all perfect.

You may see that closely held mental patterns fall away. The old ways of explaining life and relating to it don't work anymore. In the void, you may not know how to think about something. It means you are not judging. It means you are not attached to the outcome. It is a good thing. Let it be. New ways of thinking like a Divine Creator will emerge. In the meanwhile, let yourself spend time in "no thought." When you quiet your mind, you allow Divine Inspiration to speak to you. When you quiet your mind, you can hear your heart. There is great power in the mental void of "no thought."

Physically, you may experience changes. Your body is shifting to accommodate the new frequencies. Physical discomforts may surface while your body detoxifies. The clearings released dense physical drama from your cells. They need to move out of the body so your body can begin to heal and rebuild. Drink plenty of pure water to flush the toxins through. Take apple cider vinegar baths to draw out the toxins. Treat your body with respect. Re-evaluate the way you take care of yourself. Look at your eating patterns, exercise patterns and sleeping patterns. Feed your body pure, wholesome nutrition. This is a time to begin supporting the Divine Body as it regenerates.

Spiritually, you may find a void as some of your spiritual beliefs or practices may want to shift. You may actually experience a change in your spiritual guides and teachers. You are at a new - higher level of frequency and your guidance and lessons will shift to accommodate your new levels.

While you are in the void, you may experience a feeling of "I don't know what to do." The only activity that is required in void is to just take good care of yourself. Let the Divine Mother in you nurture the Divine Child — the newborn — that you are. Hold yourself in loving arms. Nurture and pamper yourself with love and tenderness. Take this time to just be — without DOING anything. Spend your time doing those things that bring you joy. For you may suddenly find that you have plenty of time on your hands. Do those things that you love, but usually never have time for. Take a nap. Take a walk. Take a bubble bath. Go to a movie. Sit by the fire and stare into it for hours.

The more love and trust you have in the void, the easier and faster your new life will appear. Listen and act on your inner guidance. Your destiny will unfold; your life's purpose will reveal itself. This will happen when there is no resistance. Resistance can look like fear and impatience. It can look like being attached and not wanting to let go of the old forms. Love yourself, trust yourself and Spirit and let go of attachment. Love, trust and let go. Love, trust and let go. Love, trust and let go. That's all you need to do in the void.

Integration Exercises

Apple Cider Vinegar Baths

After an upgrade, your system will start to shed that which is no longer in alignment with the higher frequencies and expanded consciousness. This detoxification will happen in your physical, emotional, mental and energy bodies. To help pull the toxins out of the body, take an apple cider vinegar bath every day for at least 3 days after the upgrade.

Tap into your intuition for guidance on how often to do it after that. If you are experiencing physical symptoms such as aches and pains, fatigue or flu-like symptoms, turn to the apple cider vinegar bath for support. If you have suffered from a medical condition in the past, it might surface again briefly as it moves its way out of the body for the last time.

The recipe for the bath is one half cup of apple cider vinegar in a normal size bath tub of hot water. Soak in the tub for one half hour exactly. It takes about 20 minutes for the formula to begin working. The last 10 minutes is when the toxins are being released. Bless the water and release it. Don't share the tub or the water with anyone else. A sea salt bath or a swim in the ocean may be substituted for the apple cider vinegar bath.

Integration Meditation

If you participate in a teleclass, private session or use the CDs, you will release a lot during the session. You will continue to release in the 3-7 days following the session. When you release the dense energy that no longer serves you, empty space is created. It is important to fill that empty space with higher frequencies of light. You don't want it to fill up with other peoples' stuff that is floating around in mass consciousness.

There is an Integration Meditation that is available on CD, sold separately or included in the 10-CD kit. This meditation calls in and bathes you in the higher frequencies of light. This meditation is also very good training for being able to change your frequency at will and discern the subtle differences. This meditation is 30 minutes long, so it is a perfect companion for your apple cider vinegar bath.

Journaling

Every day, or as often as possible, take time to write down how your inner and outer world is changing. Write down old **thoughts and beliefs** that come to the surface of your awareness that were unconscious before. Allow these thoughts and beliefs to voice themselves and then decide if they serve you as a Divine Human. If they do not, simply use the release technique given below.

In the same way, write down **emotions** that pop up during the integration period. You may feel strong emotional energy and not even know what memory or circumstance it is connected to. This is alright. Don't try to figure it out. Just note the emotion in your journal and then release it using the instructions below.

Also write down anything that seems like it might be a **practice exercise**. You create opportunities to practice your new consciousness. So you may create a situation that conforms to one of your old familiar patterns. You will notice that when these come up, you are much more conscious of your choices. Instead of reacting by default, you may stop and see that you now have options as to how to react. You can react from your default pattern or the new consciousness. If you react from default the first few times, don't worry. You will get more practice opportunities. You will find that you will catch and stop yourself much sooner, giving yourself opportunities to turn around the situation to a higher outcome. You will notice that you are more present in the NOW. Your practice is to more toward being free from past unconscious default behaviors and make conscious decisions in every moment.

Also make note of all the ways that the **fear of separation and abandonment** motivate your thoughts and activities. We spend so much time and energy doing things for others, not out of the generosity of our heart, as we would like to believe. But rather, because we fear disapproval and abandonment if we don't please others. This becomes a real eye-opening exercise!!! We can eliminate a lot of stress; make our lives much simpler and less hectic, if we choose to only give to others when we feel our own cup overflowing with love and joy.

If we are honest with ourselves, we will see that most people won't abandon us if we get honest and set healthy boundaries for ourselves. The people in your life who object to you honoring yourself are not coming from a place of love and honoring of themselves. You can model self-love and healthy boundaries to them. If they learn from you, fine. If not, they are not going to be able to stay in your world as you raise your vibration and expand your consciousness. Let them go in gratitude and compassion. Don't buy into their illusions of separation and abandonment.

Releasing What No Longer Serves You

Become conscious of thought patterns, beliefs, emotions and situations surfacing from the past that no longer serves you. Determine if you are ready to release them. If so, create a release command statement and use the piston breath to release.

1. Create Sacred Inner Space (see *Appendix*).

2. Recite the *I AM Invocation*: I AM All That Is. I AM All That Is. I AM All That Is. I AM Source. I AM Creator. I AM Divine Light. I AM Divine Love. I AM Divine Joy. I AM the Being of Synthesis and Fusion. I AM That I Am.

3. Then specifically state what you want to release. For example, you might become aware that you have a hidden belief that nobody could love you because you are ugly, or stupid or fat or fill in the blank. Or you might want to release anger or rage.

4. Then state what you would like to bring in to replace the thought or emotion you are releasing.

5. Do the piston breath until you feel complete. Breathe in and out through your mouth, with your tongue on the roof of your mouth. Breathe deeply into your belly, not your chest. Your belly should be going up and down like a piston. Use a moderate pace that is not so fast you will hyperventilate or so slow that you loose focus. With your imagination, you can create some kind of signal that tells you when you have completely released the mental and emotional material.

6. Ground your consciousness into your body.

7. Ground your body into the Earth.

Using the New Features

Seeing Beyond the Illusion

The ultimate illusion is that we are separate from Source, separate from each other and even separate from pieces and parts of ourselves. Yet this illusion is exactly the foundation of our reality on this planet. The other grand illusion is that we can be a victim of abandonment, betrayal or abuse.

We create our own reality. We are creating it with every thought, word and deed. We are creating it with unconscious thought patterns and beliefs as well. The main thing we want to do is to bring what is hidden into the light. We need to wake up and make conscious decisions. We want to stop creating from default mode and begin creating the reality we prefer. We can stop seeing ourselves as victims and take back our power.

With the Illusion of Separation cleared away from your DNA database, you can begin seeing beyond the illusion. The way to do this is to know that whatever situation you have before you — you created it for some reason. Underlying every creation is the advancement of your soul.

So if you have a situation or a relationship that is not how you would prefer it to be, ask yourself, "Why have I created this?" What is the person or situation mirroring back to me that I may learn from? Understand that what is happening in the world outside yourself is a reflection of what is going on inside. It is a clue to a hidden program, file or belief. Once you uncover the program or belief, you can choose to release it.

Looking at Contracts

You may assume that if someone is in your life, you have subconsciously called them to you to serve some purpose that gives you the opportunity to love another aspect of yourself. This other person plays out a role for you that mirrors what you want to learn, explore, love or release. Consider that you have attracted this particular person by subconscious agreement because they have a corresponding, complimentary lesson to learn, issue to explore, heal, love or release as well.

Sacred Union of the Male and Female

When you engage the upgrade *Sacred Union of the Inner Male/Female*, you will bring some issues and contracts to a graceful completion without the necessity for the original drama that you created for this purpose. You can use the following procedure to check what the contract is, if it is complete or what needs to happen to bring it to completion.

1. Create Sacred Inner Space (see *Appendix*).

2. Travel through the Time/Space Continuum until you come to a conference room door. Enter the conference room,

3. Recite the *I AM Invocation*: I AM All That Is. I AM All That Is. I AM All That Is. I AM Source, I AM Creator, I AM Divine Light, I AM Divine Love, I AM Divine Joy. I AM the Being of Synthesis and Fusion. I AM That I Am.

4. Invite the Librarian of your Akashic Records into the conference room. The Librarian brings your Akashic Records.

5. Ask the Librarian to show you or read to you what the contract is between you and another person.

6. Ask if the contract is complete. If not, ask what needs to happen to bring the contract to completion.

7. Feel free to ask questions of the Librarian for clarification and when you feel complete with your inquiry, thank the Librarian.

8. Bring yourself back through the Time/Space Continuum into your body.

9. Ground your consciousness in the body.

10. Ground your body into the Earth.

11. Once the contract is complete, release it using the instructions below.

Releasing Contracts

1. Create Sacred Inner Space (see *Appendix*).

2. Recite the *I AM Invocation*: I AM All That Is. I AM All That Is. I AM All That Is. I AM Source, I AM Creator, I

AM Divine Light, I AM Divine Love, I AM Divine Joy. I AM the Being of Synthesis and Fusion. I AM That I Am.

3. Give this command: I NOW command the quantum, subatomic, atomic, molecular and cellular levels; Etheric Body, Emotional Body and Mental Body, DNA, the Energy System and the time/space continuum to release and surrender all expectations, fantasies, internal dialog, emotional attachments, obsession and thoughts and contracts related to *insert name of person.* I surrender willingly and unconditionally through the Power of Divine Breath, I AM, into the integration-union: into open-hearted trust and acceptance of the Divine Plan for the sacred relationships in my life.

4. Piston breath for at least 15 minutes or longer until you feel complete then the full body breath for 5 minutes.

5. Ground your consciousness in the body.

6. Ground your body into the Earth.

Clearing the Pain Body

Upgrade Description

Eckhart Tolle's book, *The Power of Now*, inspired me to create a way to clear the Pain Body. For purposes of our discussion, we define the Pain Body as the intersection of the mental and emotional bodies where pain is stored. Painful memories (conscious and unconscious) are stored in the mental body. Unexpressed emotional pain is stored in the emotional body.

We use the red-violet ray of Passionate Compassion to transmute the emotional pain into intense self-love. The ray of Passionate Compassion is a synergistic blend of three frequencies of light. It contains the Violet Flame of Transmutation. The Violet Flame raises the frequency and purifies everything it touches. The second frequency is the Pink Ray of Compassion and the third is the Red Ray of Passion.

The Ray of Passionate Compassion can erase the memory files related to pain. Once the pain body is purified and overflowing with Passionate Compassion, we place a Platinum Ray shield around the outside of this body which prevents pain from again being stored in the Pain Body.

We call this new body *The Self-Love Body* and merge it back with our physical body, effectively wrapping ourselves in a constant blanket of Passionate Compassion.

The *Self-Love Body* will not necessary shield you from feeling pain for the rest of your life. Sadness, grief, anger do serve their purpose and are the human part of *Divine Human*. What's different is that you will not be able to STORE pain. Which means you must somehow express it as it is moving through you. In the *Using the New Features* section of this chapter you will be given tools to deal with pain at a higher level of consciousness.

You will find there is less pain in your life than before. This is the Law of Attraction at work. Like attracts like. When there is no pain stored in your system, you will not attract as many painful situations to you. You won't need to. Most often the painful situations are attracted to you in an effort to bring your attention to the pain that is inside so that you can release and heal.

Installation Command

If you choose to activate this initiation, give this command:

I AM That I AM. I AM That I AM. I AM That I AM. I now command the activation of the *Divine Human Upgrade* called *Clearing the Pain Body*. I open my heart and command all levels of my consciousness to fully to receive the gifts of this upgrade. I command my outer self to allow and embrace the needed lessons and changes this upgrade brings into my life now. I command easy, comfortable, graceful and joyful integration of the new features, higher frequencies and expanded consciousness delivered through this upgrade. So Be It. So It Is.

Integration

During the integration of this upgrade, expect that you may become aware of hidden and suppressed pain. It may surface from the past for the last time as it is forever released. You may experience emotional pain, which may or may not be connected to a specific memory.

You may become aware of all the things you do, all the energy you spend trying to avoid pain. You also may become aware of all the energy you have spent trying to hold in the pain, for fear it will escape and embarrass you.

The best way to get through this integration is to allow the pain to move through you. Don't try to hide from it, talk yourself out if it push it away or project it on to others. Acknowledge it, express it and move it through to release.

The idea is to MOVE the energy by expression. Try crying, yelling, singing or nonsensical sounds of any kind. Also consider expressing by drawing, writing, running, drumming, any physical exercise, talking into a tape recorder, dancing, doing the piston breath. Whatever works!

The first step is releasing painful thoughts and emotions from the past. When that process is complete, then stay in integrity with yourself and others by continuously communicating the truth from your heart with respect and compassion.

During the integration continue with the exercises given in the last chapter:

- Journaling
- Apple cider vinegar baths
- Integration Meditation
- Releasing What No Longer Serves You

Using the New Features

Flowing with Your Emotions

Once you have released the emotions from the past, how do you deal with the new ones that come up from now on? You've heard the term "go with the flow" and that applies here. As mentioned before, you spent a lot of energy holding on to pain and trying to avoid more pain. You will become aware of your past defense strategies and breathe a sigh of relief that you don't have to use them anymore.

With this energy freed up, you will have more energy for creative projects or for physical healing and rejuvenation. Much of your suppressed pain has been trapped in your body as disease. With the painful memories and suppressed emotions released, your body is free to restore itself to balance, harmony and health.

Imagine that you receive word that a dear friend or family member has just passed away. Will you feel sadness or grief? Of course! Allow yourself to feel it. Let it be a wave that washes over you. Open your heart wide to it. If you offer the sadness or grief no resistance, it will move through you like a wave. It may feel like it hits you in your heart, open to it, welcome it, express it and it will move right through you and out the other side.

At times I have felt intense emotional energy. It seems to come out of nowhere. I don't know if it is mine or just a wave floating by from the collective consciousness. It isn't associated within anything that is going on in my present reality. I can't even identify the kind of emotion it is such as fear or grief. It is just intensely dense emotional energy.

There have been times when it shows up as a pain in the middle of my back, corresponding to the back of my heart chakra. I lie down, give myself the instruction to open my heart wide and let it pass through without any resistance. I breathe deeply. Within moments, it is gone. Visualize intense emotional energy washing through you like a wave. This is simple, but it works.

Love Laser

The Love Laser is a powerful tool to cut through the veils around the hearts and minds of those who believe in the Illusion of Separation. The Illusion of Separation causes men to turn against each other and forget the unity and truth of our Oneness. There is only love. All else is an illusion created by the mind of man as a game board to play in this 3-D holographic world of form.

The Love Laser is a specific frequency of light energy that is focused and concentrated, like a light saber or a sword. It is projected from your heart center into the heart center of another. The light beam contains the transmuting characteristics of the Violet Flame, the ruby red Ray of Passion and the pink Ray of Compassion. The Platinum Ray surrounds the red/violet ray, which further defines, focuses and accelerates the power of the beam. Anyone who is willing can take up the Love Laser to help eradicate the fear-based Illusion of Separation.

The effects of the Love Laser benefit both the giver and the receiver, which will:

- Open them to feel Passionate Compassion for themselves and all others
- Remember the truth — we are all Divine
- Recognize the Illusion of Separation and embrace the unity of All That Is

Send the Love Laser to:

1. Anyone you know personally (including yourself) who is feeling or causing pain due to the feeling of separation from Source, themselves or from others.

2. Our leaders, so they may make wise decisions based in love and compassion rather than fear and vengeance.

3. Blessed Mother Earth to help her transmute the battle energy that is held in the land.

4. Following are the instructions on how to receive and use the Love Laser.

5. Read the transmission entitled *Radiant One* (Foreword of this book). As you read it, write down all your feelings and thoughts as you realize that this message applies to you. It might trigger fear, rage, guilt, self-judgment or denial. Allow the shadow issues to come up and reveal themselves in the light. Feel these emotions and acknowledge them.

6. Write down all the thoughts and feelings that come up when you realize that this message also applies to everyone else on this planet.

7. Understand this. The people who participate in terrorism have forgotten Who They Really Are. They passionately believe in the Illusion of Separation. They want to control the masses, because they feel out of control. Some are passionate about amassing fortunes because they fear lack and don't trust the abundance of All That Is. Some passionately fear victimhood, so they victimize others to cover up their fear. Some passionately fear freedom. To integrate the polarities of fear and love, we must match their level of passion with our own. We must passionately send them the highest frequency, which is compassion. This is the biggest wakeup call they can receive. This will awaken them to Who They Really Are. When they remember, they will lay down their weapons.

8. To be initiated as a Love Laser Peacemaker, state this command with intense intention and feeling. I AM now commanding the Initiation of the Beam of Passionate Compassion.

9. See, feel, and know that a beam of light coming in through the top of your head and moving all the way through your body and continuing down into the Heart of the Earth. This beam of light is the color red-violet. It comes from Source.

10. As this beam moves through you, start breathing it in. See, feel, imagine, and command that it enter all of the cells of your body. Continue to expand the beam of light until it fills up your physical body. Then expand it more to fill up your energy field. Fill yourself to overflowing. Feel a fountain of red-violet energy coming out of your head and flowing down your body and into the atmosphere around you.

11. Now see a beam of this red/violet light coming out of the center of your chest. This is your heart center/chakra.

12. Surround the red-violet ray with the Platinum Ray. This is the Love Laser.

13. Give this command, "I AM now commanding the Love Laser to cut through the veils of separation surrounding the heart of all beings who believe in the Illusion of Separation."

14. See the Laser filling the hearts of all those who believe in separation. Watch, imagine, and command that the platinum coated red-violet ray spreads all the way through their bodies and into the Heart of the Earth. Watch, imagine, and command that the laser fills them to overflowing like a fountain.

15. From your heart, send this communication through the laser beam, "You are Divine Light. You are Divine Love. We are all One." Say this three times.

16. Now see their Higher Self recognize the truth and take over the mantra: I AM Divine Light. I AM Divine Love. I AM Divine Unity. I AM That I AM." Hear and feel this mantra being repeated by the Higher Self over and over again until the ego hears it and begins to remember the truth of it and starts to chant it.

17. Now see this overflowing energy moving all over the surface of the Earth and filling up the energy body of the Earth.

18. Feel the energy in you, in the Earth and in all beings.

19. Feel the Oneness.

20. Feel the Awakening.

21. Feel the gratitude and give thanks.

22. Command: It is done. So Be It! So It Is!

This activation is most powerful when used in groups. Use your own intuition to guide you in doing this as often as it feels of service. It will be of the highest good to all concerned if you do it every time you feel fear, anger, grief or despair.

Out'ta Your Mind

Upgrade Description

In this initiation, the first thing we do is bring your Divine Plan right into your solar plexus and anchor it there. This blueprint contains information on *Who You Really Are*, where you came from, where you've been and what you've been doing and your Divine Plan for expressing yourself as a *Divine Human.* It also contains the records of your Family of Light, who are actually other aspects of you in the Higher Dimensions. This is your true identity.

We introduce you to the Deva of your mind-created identity, a.k.a. Ego. With the new *Divine Human* identity installed, your ego sees this as an upgrade and is willing to uninstall the old identify. The ego is honored in a promotion ceremony and given the new position as Advisor of Integrity. The Advisor of Integrity's new job is to follow your Divine Plan using the new talents, wisdom and knowledge of your *Divine Human* identity.

Then we command the purging of mind-created self-image based on limited perception within the polarity grid.

We command the release of all judgments, rules, strategies and the supporting documentation related to the mind-created self-image. Your mind is then reprogrammed with a new master command, which is to read the Divine Plan and keep you in alignment with it. You release judgment and replace it with discernment. In each moment, your mind is guiding you to stay in impeccable integrity with your own Divine Plan (Divine Will).

We bring in the records of any divine wisdom, knowledge, skills, talents and creative gifts that you have accumulated in parallel lifetimes that might be used for creative expression, aligned with your Divine Plan for this lifetime.

When you agreed to incarnate on planet earth, you accepted this mind software, just like putting on a virtual reality game helmet. The software was preprogrammed with the rules and structure for this 3D holographic polarity game. The rules of this game are not universal law. They are made up rules of order for the Polarity Integration Game. You can choose to uninstall the made up rules of the polarity integration game and install Divine Plan for Paradise on Earth.

Then we address the areas of judgment, guilt and fear. The judgments programs you have accumulated are related to the made up rules of the polarity integration game and your mind-created identity. The fear and guilt programming kicks in whenever your thoughts or actions go beyond the limits of the game rules and judgment programs. Fear and guilt are very effective programs for keeping you in alignment with your mind-created identity and the rules of the game. Well of course, we can see that this programming is now obsolete. We can uninstall this programming.

Judgment is replaced with discernment. It is for you to discern in every moment if you are in alignment, in integrity, with your own *Divine Human* Blueprint. That is the only question you need ever ask. As for everyone else, it's up to them to act in accordance with their programming — whatever that is at the moment. It is none of your business what other people think, feel or do. The only thing that matters is that you stay in alignment with your own *Divine Human* Blueprint. Non-judgment of yourself and other + allowance for all others to be as they are = compassion.

Now you will find that as a compassionate *Divine Human*, you will be overflowing with love and joy. Because you stay in impeccable integrity with your Divine Plan, you would never impose your will or your plan on anyone else. So others come to trust your integrity, your open heartedness, your generosity.

By the way, your Divine Plan is already in alignment with the Divine Plan of The Creative Source for life on this planet. To stay in alignment with your Divine Plan is surrendering to the Creative Source's Plan. Your Divine Plan is a puzzle piece in the overall plan of the Creator. It is a merging of "Thy Plan" and "My Plan." This merging has been discussed here in its more technical aspects, yet it is one of the highest spiritual principals emphasized in every spiritual tradition.

Installation Command

If you choose to activate this initiation, give this command:

I AM That I AM. I AM That I AM. I AM That I AM. I now command the activation of the *Divine Human Upgrade* called *Out'ta Your Mind*. I open my heart and command all levels of my consciousness to fully to receive the gifts of this upgrade. I command my outer self to allow and embrace the needed lessons and changes this upgrade brings into my life now. I command easy, comfortable, graceful and joyful integration of the new features, higher frequencies and expanded consciousness delivered through this upgrade. So Be It. So It Is.

Integration

Integration of this upgrade will be similar to the other two. You will continue to become aware of old programming that no longer serves you as a *Divine Human*. Continue with the same Integration Exercises:

- Journaling
- Apple cider vinegar baths
- Integration Meditation
- Releasing What No Longer Serves You

Using the New Features

Consulting the Advisor of Integrity

If you receive this upgrade via a teleclass or CD, you will be introduced to your Advisor of Integrity and given a practice lesson in communicating.

Your Advisor of Integrity has been given access to your Divine Plan and can read what's there. It is your Advisor's job to keep you in alignment with your Divine Plan in each moment. Only one question remains, "Is this in alignment with my Divine Plan?"

For example, imagine you get invited to a social event after work. You would ask, "Is it in alignment with my Divine Plan to go to this event tonight?"

Depending on the answer, you might ask another question for more clarity. If the answer is no, you might ask, "what activity would be in alignment with my Divine Plan tonight?" You might be told to go home and rest.

Or if the answer was yes, you might ask, "What opportunities should I be aware of during this event?" In the beginning you might just get yes or no answers. But after strengthening the relationship with your Advisor of Integrity, you may be able to hear more robust answers.

This is a relationship. Like any relationship, you have to nurture it. If you forget about your Advisor of Integrity, it might take a while for you both to build trust. Regardless of whether you communicate or not, your Advisor will be carrying out the program to align with your Divine Plan.

Downloading Programs

You can download programs that will give you any knowledge, wisdom or skill you would like. No longer are you limited by what your mind has to learn.

In the first Matrix Movie, Neo was being chased by men who wanted to kill him. His only getaway opportunity was a helicopter. He didn't know how to operate the helicopter, but he had a mind to mind linkup with his team in another dimension. He contacted them and told them the make and model of the helicopter and they instantly downloaded the program, complete with training exercises directly into Neo's mind. Within seconds he could operate the helicopter and make his getaway.

To download a program:

1. Prepare by getting some colored drawing instruments like crayons, pencils, paints or chalks. Get some drawing or painting paper.

2. On the back side of the paper, write down specifically what you would like to be able to do. List all the specifications until you have a full description.

3. Connect with your spiritual team. Most people have an Angelic Team and a Galactic Team.

4. Give the command for the downloading of the program.

5. On the other side of the paper, while the program is downloading, open yourself to receive it and bring it through your body into the physical world by drawing it on paper. You don't need to be a fine artist to do this. Just let the energy move your hand. Grab different colors intuitively. The end result doesn't have to look like anything recognizable in form. The energy is grounded into to the paper and you can use the drawing to reconnect and realign with the program in the future.

6. Ask your team how long before the program will be fully operational. It may take days or weeks to become operational.

7. Ask your team what you need to do to integrate the new program. Write down the directions your team gives you and follow them.

8. Use the drawing to align with the program until it becomes fully operational.

I downloaded a program for accelerated writing and drawing. This book seems to be writing itself. My hand can hardly keep up with the images that flow so quickly through my pencils and paints when I draw. I downloaded a program for singing Light Language and am amazed at the beautiful sounds coming out of my mouth. It works!

Telepathic Communication

The Love Laser introduced in the last chapter is also a very useful communication device. Remember it is a heart to heart connection. You can use it to:

- Connect and communicate with other people, through the heart space.

- Connect and communicate with plants, minerals, animals and the consciousness of anything in form.

- Connect and communicate with any being in the Spirit Realm and other dimensions.

Please exercise honor and respect when using this new feature. You are not allowed to violate anyone's private thoughts or space. This is not about reading another persons mind. It is setting a communication bridge, just like a telephone.

Before connecting, send out a telepathic calling card, introducing yourself and asking for permission to communicate. Use discernment! Please realize that what you put out comes back to you — instantly. So the Golden Rule applies more than ever.

Never reach out to communicate when you are in fear, guilt or judgment. Clear and calm yourself before establishing communication with anybody.

By the same token, it is your right to establish healthy boundaries for yourself. If others are not honoring you or telepathic protocol, compassionately let them know right away. This is new for all of us and a period of adjustment will occur before we get used to this new level of communication. Compassion is called for.

Embracing Abundance

Upgrade Description

I have learned that we have an implanted thought pattern that makes us believe that money is a separate and different kind of energy from all other energy. This is an illusion. We separated it and put it in a separate undefined box in our mind. This is reflected outwardly as putting money in the bank. This stops the flow of money in and out of our lives. In this upgrade, we restore the flow. We also release feelings, attitudes, beliefs related to lack and limitation. We install the Advisor of Abundance to creatively redeem all abundance you may have deflected by the implanted thought pattern.

We also clear past life vows and agreements that no longer serve you. Many of these, like the vow of poverty, were taken because we honestly believed self-denial would bring us closer to God. Signs of a past life vow problem are:

- If you have tried affirmations persistently and sincerely with no apparent result.

- If you are acting in ways that you know are not in your best interest but you just "cannot help it."

- If you are acting in ways that "do not make sense" in the context of your life now.

We will be clearing vows of poverty, chastity, self-sacrifice, celibacy/separation, silence/self-denial, suffering/self-punishment, salvation and obedience.

Installation Command

If you choose to activate this initiation, give this command:

> I AM That I AM. I AM That I AM. I AM That I AM. I now command the activation of the *Divine Human Upgrade* called *Embracing Abundance*. I open my heart and command all levels of my consciousness to fully receive the gifts of this upgrade. I command my outer self to allow and embrace the needed lessons and changes this upgrade brings into my life now. I command easy, comfortable, graceful and joyful integration of the new features, higher frequencies and expanded consciousness delivered through this upgrade. So Be It. So It Is.

Integration

Integration of this upgrade will be similar to the others. You will continue to become aware of old programming that know longer serves you as a *Divine Human*. Continue with the same Integration Exercises:

- Journaling
- Apple cider vinegar baths
- Integration Meditation
- Releasing What No Longer Serves You

This upgrade, for some people, can be the most uncomfortable one to integrate. Since money has been linked with survival in our minds, when things shift in the way our abundance flows to us, it can be very scary.

> Our human egos have manipulated us by perpetuating the illusion that our physical bodies are all that we are and that the physical plane of Earth is all that exists. These distorted beliefs caused Humanity to develop a poverty consciousness of lack and limitation. This motivated our human egos to obsessively and compulsively fight to gratify our physical senses. Greed, selfishness, war, hatred, fear, crime, corruption, intolerance and every other abuse of power can be traced back to the poverty consciousness of our fear-based human egos.
>
> Patricia Cota-Robles, http://www.1spirit.com/eraofpeace/

Embracing Abundance

Together we have co-created a reality that enslaves us at every turn — especially economically. We have enslavement grids of thought that have built a very solid structure around our reality. The structure has been closing in on us in recent years, so much so that we are being suffocated by it.

As of May 3, 2005 an Emancipation Matrix was anchored on to the planet. It is a part of the Paradise Blueprint. In our new fifth dimensional reality, we will all be abundant. Everything we want and need, will be instantly manifested for us. We will not have to "work for a living." We will have lots of leisure time to pursue that which brings us joy.

The Emancipation Matrix is far more free and flexible than our current structures. It is anchored to the earth at about eight specific points. Yet, between these anchor points, it flaps free in the wind like a ribbon-like net. Since this Emancipation Matrix has anchored, the enslavement grids are now beginning to dissolve. There are temporary transitional structures that are being put in place to bridge us from the very structured reality to the more flexible, flowing reality of the fifth dimension. This transitional bridge structure is necessary to prevent the all-out chaos that could occur if the enslavement grids were just yanked away.

Some examples of enslavement grids: employment, pensions, government, taxes, insurance, credit, debt, interest, religion, media, education, allopathic healthcare, etc.

We already see that these systems, that were supposed to make us feel safe and secure, are falling apart. They don't work anymore. It was bound to happen, because we gave our power away to these systems, believing that our security was outside of ourselves.

So before these systems fall apart completely, take your power back and learn how to be a conscious creator of your reality. Practice and master conscious co-creation. Magnetize your abundance to you. By the time these systems fall apart completely, and they will, you will have created your own security in your ability to manifest.

There are teachers whose main focus is abundance and prosperity. So I will refer you to them rather than try to jam all of that into this book. Bryan DeFlores, is one of the best examples of someone who has mastered the new prosperity blueprint. I recommend his manual, *The Golden Age Business Plan* at www.bryandeflores.com.

Another teacher that I recommend is Elyse Hope Killoran at www.choosingprosperity.com. She has developed a wonderful on-line virtual reality game that helps you to start flowing prosperity in a virtual dimension if you don't have something to start with in this dimension. The mind doesn't know the difference between physical and imagination. You can reprogram your mind using your imagination and it will work.

A prosperity teacher that understands that the default programming of your mind determines your reality is Harv Eker, author of the best selling book, *Secrets of a Millionaire Mind*. He has figured out the exact mental blueprint for the millionaire mind and promises that if you attend one of his 3-day intensive workshops, you will walk out with your money blueprint upgraded permanently.

After you have developed your Golden Business Plan and have started money flowing, you can refer to Shared Vision Network at www.sharedvisionnetwork.com. This is a network of entrepreneurs who have already left their employers and are enjoying their prosperity by making a business out of what they truly love. They are following their passion. They offer all kinds of teleclasses for learning how to create, run and grow your own business.

Using the New Features

Manifesting From the Heart

How is manifesting from your heart different from manifesting from your mind? Why would you want to change the way you've been manifesting? When you manifest from the heart, you connect with our own Divine Human identity and your own Divine Plan. Your Divine Plan is usually much grander, much richer, and much more abundant than what your mind can conceive. Why? Because your mind may be holding on to limiting beliefs of lack, fear or insecurity. Or maybe you can't imagine it, because it is so outside of your experience.

When you connect with your Divine Human identity, you will remember that you are a powerful creator. You realize that everything in creation is already created. It is your mind that holds the notion of time. When your mind thinks about what it would like to create, looks around in the physical world and doesn't see it, you believe it doesn't exist. And yet it does exist — somewhere.

Let's look a little deeper into the function of the mind as it relates to your experience as a spiritual being. Your mind slows down the flow of creation moving through your consciousness. It slows it down so that you can take a closer look. Just like changing the speed of a movie, it slows down so you can look at it frame by frame. The mind does this so that it can understand and learn from your experience. It can observe relationships between cause and effect. It stores the perceptions and beliefs it has about what it observes. These perceptions and beliefs are not truth; they are the mind's interpretation of what it is observing. After noticing a similar cause-effect relationship a few times, the mind will establish a rule (belief) and treat it as the truth about how the world works. These beliefs establish a framework for future mind-generated creations. Your Divine Human identity does not have this limitation. It has the freedom to create more wonderful things than your mind can imagine.

Another function of the mind is as a filter. There is so much going on in creation. The mind filters out most of it so you can focus on a few core objectives in this physical world. When the mind receives too much input from the senses, it overloads, gets confused and cannot understand the input.

One thing happening on our planet is that our consciousness is expanding and allowing more experience and more information to run through it at the same time. That is why we have a sense that time is speeding up and so much more happens in a day. Time hasn't sped up. Our consciousness has expanded and more is moving through it.

When your consciousness expands completely, you will be aware of everything at once and the illusion of time will dissolve. That was what the Mayans were referring to when they predicted the end of time. It's not the end of the world. It's when our consciousness expands to include simultaneous everything.

Simultaneous everything already exists; our minds just aren't hip to it yet.

Everything in creation already exists. This is a planet of free choice. For every little decision you make, there is one 'you' that plays out one decision on this physical plane and an alternate you that plays out the other decision in some other dimension or physical plane. Richard Bach wrote a great book that illustrates this called *One*. I highly recommend it for *Divine Human* Creator Gods and Goddesses who want to understand simultaneous everything — or One.

The big decision for *Divine Human*s creating Paradise on Earth is "of all the possible realities that already exist, which one do I want to bring into this physical plane to experience?" As *Divine Human* creators, it is our privilege and responsibility to make those decisions. How do we choose and how do we bring it into this physical plane?

Once we reach a certain point in our evolution of consciousness, it will be automatic. But for now what I propose is a transition plan while we are bridging the two worlds between third dimensional reality and fifth dimensional reality. We can call this part of the Rainbow Bridge Plan. By the way — 'simultaneous everything' is a characteristic of the higher dimensional realities.

Let's use a metaphor for a moment. Given that all of creation is already created, let's imagine that for every possible reality, a movie is already made that you can look at. Imagine that you are going to walk into the Rainbow Bridge DVD Library to pick out a movie. Well you can imagine how many DVDs there are. How will you choose one?

There is a librarian there to help you. The Librarian asks, "How would you like to **feel**?" Feelings are in the heart, not the head. What are the feeling characteristics of the experience you are choosing?

Back to the movie metaphor... Currently when you walk into a video store, the movies are usually organized in categories. Are you in the mood to experience a drama, an action film, a romantic comedy, a thriller? I usually prefer romantic comedies myself. But there are lots of people who really like a good, bloody, shoot 'em up action adventure and even those who really like to get their adrenaline going with a horror flick.

Who am I to judge what other people may want to experience — either in a movie or in their physical reality? This is where compassion comes in. Compassion is non-judgment. Compassion is realizing that we are all *Divine Human*s creating our own reality — either consciously or unconsciously. It's not up to me to look at somebody else and say, you look like you are suffering, so I'm going to take you out of your melodrama and drag you into my romantic comedy.

No. As *Divine Human*s, we see the divinity in all others and know that at some level of their being, for whatever reason, they chose the exact movie they are starring in. As teachers of New Energy, it's possible that our laughter will be so joyous that others might notice. When they say to you, "You seem to be having great fun in your romantic comedy while I'm suffering through yet another melodrama. How can I star in my own romantic comedy?" Then, and only then, are they ready.

Rest assured, if you clear yourself of your limited, fear-based beliefs and manifest from the heart, you can star in any kind of movie you want. You will attract actors who want to play in the same kind of movie you do. The ones who are still choosing melodrama will not even notice you. If you don't release your limiting fear-based beliefs, your mind will continue to filter out the information and opportunities that would allow you to manifest your heart's desire.

Back to the Rainbow Bridge DVD Library... The librarian guides you into some clarity about what you would like to feel in this experience. That feeling, the frequency of it, sets up a resonant frequency which automatically seeks out the movie in the library that matches it. The librarian locates the movie and puts it in the playback machine for you to view.

You watch the movie and of course, it is much more wonderful than you could have imagined — because your Divine Self wrote the script. Now you have a choice whether you want to leave this movie in the Rainbow Bridge Library, which is unmanifested reality, or to bring it into this physical plane so you can actively participate in it.

That is the difference between fantasizing and manifesting. You are viewing a potential reality in both cases. When you fantasize, your mind says, this is not possible in my life, so I'll just enjoy it here on the movie screen of my mind. Every time you fantasize, you give more energy to this alternative reality; you keep it alive for some alternative you, choosing not to anchor it in this physical plane.

If you really want to experience that movie in this physical plane, you need to go a little further. To choose and anchor the movie, again, get into the feeling of it. Allow your heart to feel the emotional experience. Feel it in rich sensual detail as if it is already happening. Feel the joy. Feel the gratitude. Then send the movie into the Earth. Ground it in this physical reality.

In the New Energy, for *Divine Human*s, when you have freed yourself from the fear-based matrix, manifesting your heart's desire is that easy.

A word to the wise... For those more complex, multi-faceted life change manifestations, you must continue to nurture your creation by giving it energy and staying open to allowing it to unfold. Once your manifestation begins taking form, you must employ Divine Integrity and Divine Discipline.

Divine Integrity means checking with your own Divine Plan every time you have to make a decision. For example, say that you are invited to a social gathering after work. You are tired and would really like to go home and crawl into bed. Divine Discipline comes in and says, "Always check with your Divine Plan."

In one case, you may look at your Divine Plan (looking into a simultaneous now moment that hasn't yet moved through your consciousness) and see that there is a person at this social gathering who can open the door to an important opportunity that will bring you one of the heart's desires. To be in Divine Integrity with your Divine Plan, you would employ Divine Discipline and go to the party, even though you are tired. Once you make that decision, your Divine Self will supply the energy you need to go to the party, have a good time and make that important connection.

Another evening, your Divine Plan tells you that nothing of consequence can happen at this gathering and it would serve you better to go home and get some rest.

Divine Discipline may also be employed to redirect your mind when it introduces fears and self-doubts about your ability to manifest your dreams. Catch yourself and stop the negative mind chatter. Then consciously bring your attention, and creation, into your heart again. Feel the joy and gratitude, knowing that it is already taking form. When you can feel the joy and gratitude in your emotional body, send it into the Earth.

If you don't employ Divine Discipline and Divine Integrity, your creation will manifest — in some other dimension and you may not get to experience it in this physical plane of existence.

Simple Creation Method

Here is the method for manifesting simple creations. Bring your attention to your heart center in the middle of your chest. Picture a large figure 8, the infinity sign, superimposed over your body. The center, where the two loops come together, is in your heart center. The bottom loop is at the level of your feet, relaxing on the surface of the Earth. We are going to throw the top loop up into the Rainbow Bridge DVD Library — which is unmanifested reality, and like a lasso we will pull down your creation (represented by a DVD) from that dimension into this physical plane.

Imagine you are on the way to a meeting and encounter a traffic jam. You realize this will make you late for your appointment. In your mind, get clear about what you would like to see happen. It could be something like this: You are arriving at the meeting location, feeling relaxed and confident and are greeted warmly and told "what perfect timing you have!"

Now, looking up (unmanifested reality feels like up to me), enclose your creation in a sphere of compassion. Then send the top loop of your figure 8 up, lasso the sphere and then bring it down into your heart. When the sphere of compassion that contains your creation is in your heart, feel how relaxed you are, feel the gratitude that you didn't keep your friend waiting. Allow yourself to feel your friend's gratitude at your perfect timing. Allow yourself to feel the joy that your manifestation took form so easily. Energize the creation in the sphere with this emotional energy from your heart and then send it into the core of Mother Earth. The momentum of the sphere will stretch the bottom loop of the figure 8 all the way to the Heart of Blessed Mother Earth. Give her a moment to read the sphere, and then use the bottom loop of the figure 8 to bring the sphere back up into your heart. Then relax and drive with confidence to your appointment.

This simple method only takes a few seconds. The results will astound you. It's fascinating to watch how creative Mother Earth, your Divine Self and the other unseen forces are that bring your manifestations to you. It could happen in an unlimited number of ways, so don't try to figure it out. Let go of the HOW. Totally let go of it. You have to let go of it in order to allow it to happen in the easiest, most creative way. Surrender to the fact that your mind doesn't know HOW to do it. But your Divine Self does. Allow your Divine Self to do its job. Have fun and enjoy the magic.

Multi-Faceted Creations

The process for manifesting multi-faceted, life-changing creations is really the same. Yet, the human mind, being as curious as it is, likes to know in rich detail what it is creating. The only difference from simple creations is you spend a little more time looking at what your Divine Self has designed for you.

For instructional purposes, I'll step you through the process using "manifesting a *Sacred Union Partner*" as an example. A *Sacred Union Partner* doesn't necessarily have to be a romantic partner. A *Sacred Union Partnership* is any relationship where you dedicate the synergy of your combined *Divine Human* energies to serve the Divine Plan together. In addition to Casey, I have several other *Sacred Union Partnerships* in my life with people who are committed to sharing the *Sacred Union* teachings with the world.

For your convenience, I have produced a CD called *Manifesting from the Heart* which guides you into a deep theta state of consciousness that makes it easier to access your creative and Divine Self. You can use the CD to manifest anything your want. It guides you through the following process, allowing you to "fill in the blank" with whatever you want to manifest.

Create a comfortable, relaxed, safe and loving space that will support you in taking a journey inside yourself. Prepare your space. I recommend you make this a very sacred time. After all you are creating your version of Paradise on Earth. Pretty important stuff. Make sure you won't be disturbed or interrupted. Make sure the environment is one that promotes a sense of safety and relaxation.

Have a notebook and writing instrument handy. You will be observing a movie that is already made; observing it from many different aspects and you will be taking notes about what you see. Don't get discouraged if you don't really "see" this like a movie in the screen of your mind. Some people have an inner sight; some don't. I don't myself. I am clairsentient, which means information comes to me in non-visual ways. Suddenly I just know something that I didn't know before. Then I am able to translate this knowing into a visual image and can use visual words to describe my knowing. Some of you may hear yourself describing the movie instead of really seeing it. Some will even be able to taste, smell and touch within the experience. Whatever ways your creativity speaks to you, go with it. Just start taking notes and the impressions will start flowing.

In this creative visualization, most often, you will be passively observing and taking notes. Don't let your mind think about what it would like and then create images. Instead, focus on feelings you would like to have (staying in the heart) and then observe what your Divine Self presents to you.

First, spend some time getting clear about how you want to **FEEL** when this *Sacred Union Partner* is in your life. Write down what you feel when you are in this partnership. What does it feel like the first time you meet? What does it feel like when you are getting to know each other? What does it feel like when you wake up in the morning and your partner is there? What does if feel like when you play together? What does it feel like when you relax together? What does it feel like when you work together on a creative project? What does it feel like when you come together after being apart for a while? What does it feel like when you have a major life challenge to face together? What does it feel like when you are speaking your truth and it makes your partner uncomfortable? Write down these feelings and take them with you when you go to meet the Librarian at the Rainbow Bridge DVD Library.

This is about using your imagination as a creative tool. However you do it, get yourself into a relaxed and receptive state of being. Then imagine moving up a stairway or elevator and arriving at the Rainbow Bridge DVD Library. Greet the Librarian and feel the welcome, unconditional love and support. The Librarian asks you what you want to manifest and how you would like to feel when it has already taken form. Read what you have written and allow yourself to feel those emotions as much as possible. The Librarian does something (allow your imagination to just witness what it is) that reads the frequencies coming from your feelings and then selects a DVD from the Library that matches it.

The Librarian puts the DVD in a playback device and you watch or experience it. The Librarian operates the controls and adjusts the movie so you can look at it from several different perspectives. The perspectives I use come from the Feng Shui Bagau. I will list them here. Make notes about what you experience while focusing on each of these categories. I will continue to move with the example of manifesting a *Sacred Union Partner* and relate each category to that kind of manifestation. But you can substitute any other manifestation you want.

Relationship/Love/Marriage:

In this category, we can look at how the *Sacred Union Partnership* expresses itself in form. One example is the traditional form of marriage where you live together full time and share your financial resources. That form doesn't work for many partnerships. Move past the limits and patterns of the past. Allow your creativity to present to you what form will best support your *Sacred Union Partnership*. Write down what you experience when focusing on this category.

Children/Creativity/Creative Projects:

How are your children, or your partner's children, or children you might have together affecting the relationship? How are the children affected by the relationship? Are other children brought into your life? This category also treats creativity and creative projects as "your children." How are your creative projects affected by this partnership? How is the partnership affected by the projects? Do your combined talents cause you to enter in to new kinds of creative projects with your partner?

Benefactors/Helpful, Supportive People:

Who steps forward as benefactors or supporters in this relationship? Maybe your partner brings new support into your life. Maybe your partnership creates new projects for you to work on together and new supporters show up. Observe what shows up when you ask the Librarian to focus on "Benefactors."

Career/Life Path:

Currently your career and life path might not be the same thing. Your life path is your Divine Plan for how you will express yourself creatively as a *Divine Human*. How does this *Sacred Union Partnership* affect your career or life path? How is your career or life path affected by your partnership?

Skills/Knowledge/Wisdom:

What skills/knowledge/wisdom do you and your partner bring to this relationship and how are they employed? What new skills/knowledge/wisdom will come in to fulfill your Divine Plan together? Remember, as you integrate your own *Sacred Union*, you will be merging with other aspects of yourself in other times or other dimensions. They may bring new skills/knowledge/wisdom for expression in this embodiment. What does your creativity show you when you ask the Librarian to focus on skills/knowledge/wisdom?

Foundation/Structure:

How does this partnership affect your lifestyle? How is your lifestyle affected by the partnership? Do you stay in the same location? Do you travel? Is there a shift in work and leisure time? What do you do with your leisure time? Is there a different foundation or structure to your life?

Prosperity/Abundance:

How is your abundance and prosperity affected by this partnership? How is the partnership affected by abundance and prosperity? What are the sources of your abundance and prosperity? How do you express your abundance and prosperity? What else can the Librarian show you about how your abundance and prosperity is enhanced through this partnership?

Fame/Reputation:

This category deals with how the outside world sees you, both as an individual and in this partnership. How is your reputation affected by the partnership? How do your individual reputations affect the partnership? Does your relationship invite the outside world in? Or do the two of you prefer a more private, reclusive reputation.

Health/Heart:

This last category deals with your health. How is your health affected by this partnership? How does the partnership affect your health? Is there anything you need to do to bring your body into a healthier state so you can fully enjoy the benefits of this partnership? How do you and partner prioritize health in your lives?

After you complete your list, if you have any other questions, ask the Librarian to tune into a view that will give the answers. Sample of additional questions:

Show me how I first meet this partner? When do we meet? Show me moving along the timeline from now until full manifestation. What opportunities present themselves? What doors open up? How does the transition go between here and there? What needs to happen to bring this into form? What Divine Discipline must I employ to bring this into form in the given timeline?

When you have all of your questions answered, then you need to decide if you want to bring this partner into your manifested reality or not. If so, inform the Librarian of your decision. Imagine the Librarian holding the DVD that represents the holographic reality you want to bring into form. The Librarian creates a Sphere of Compassion, places the DVD inside this pink sphere, and then places the sphere above your head.

Create a figure 8, the infinity sign, making sure the two loops cross at your heart. Then send the top loop of your figure 8 up, lasso the sphere and then bring it down into your heart. When the *Sphere of Compassion* that contains your creation is in your heart, get into the feeling. Knowing that in this moment you are manifesting your *Sacred Union Partnership*, feel the joy and gratitude. Feel all those feelings you began your creation with. Feel the joy when you first realize that this is the partner you have manifested. Feel your gratitude when you laugh together. Feel what its like to see each other after being apart. Feel it as if it is happening now. BE THERE NOW and feel the joy and gratitude.

Energize the creation in the sphere with this emotional energy from your heart and then send it into the core of Mother Earth. The momentum of the sphere will stretch the bottom loop of the figure 8 all the way to the Heart of Blessed Mother Earth. Give her a moment to read the sphere, and then use the bottom loop of the figure 8 to bring the sphere back up into your heart. Feel Mother Earth's blessings and support and then send the sphere off into the Universe to gather form. Just let it go. Let it float away out of sight. Relax in the knowing that IT IS DONE. LET IT GO. Forget about it. Letting it go with full confidence that it will manifest is one of the most important aspects of manifesting. If you hold on to it with worry, doubt and unworthiness, you block its manifestation.

The Sphere of Compassion helps protect your creation from worry, doubt and unworthiness thoughts and energies. But you must also employ Divine Discipline and do your part to stay open to the miracles that can unfold to bring you your heart's desire. Stay present in the NOW as much as possible. Check with your inner guidance whenever you have a decision to make. Listen to your intuition.

Integrating Polarity

Upgrade Description

In this initiation, we merge with Source, travel multi-dimensionally and remember how and why we co-created the Polarity Integration Game. With this remembrance and understanding, we can finally integrate polarity and duality. We come to a state of compassion and gratitude for our co-creative journey. Finally we can "be in the world, but not of it."

Every time we experience a trauma (mental, emotional, physical or spiritual), we potentially lose a soul or heart essence fragment. This is a self-protect mechanism. It allows us to not be totally present at the time of impact, minimizing the pain. Healers of all indigenous cultures understood this. Whenever members of their village would experience a trauma, the healer, often with the support of the whole community would perform a soul retrieval. This process calls back lost soul and heart essence that has gone into other dimensions for safety. It's time to let the lost fragments know it's safe to return. We will gracefully bring them back into *Sacred Union* with the body.

My creation story

This upgrade is the combination of two spontaneous initiation experiences that I went through. I'll share with you my first-hand experience with this. In May 2003, I had been performing an invocation calling in the Divine Mother to merge with my physical body and express more fully through me. My request was answered during a meditative journey that projected me spontaneously into one of the most amazing experiences of my life.

My consciousness was suddenly racing out of my body and out into the cosmos. Yet I was still very much aware of my physical body and its sensations. My consciousness moved out beyond all form and into a vast sea of nothingness. In a sense, it felt like my whole feeling body expanded to include all of this nothingness. For a moment there was stillness. At one level, it felt like a human moment that passed quickly. But there was another sense that this moment had lasted for billions of years.

From the stillness, I noticed movement, an undulating rhythmic movement. Somehow I recognized this movement as my feeling body, which seemed so vast; I couldn't even know its limits. Yet it seemed that somewhere way off, there were edges that defined me from the nothingness.

Suddenly there was a consciousness with no body, but intense focus and attraction to my movement. The enormity of the sudden attention and focus was so overwhelming. I could not resist. It would not be denied. There was no to time to decide or allow. Surrender happened. When it penetrated its consciousness into my moving body, when we merged, there were tremendous spasms and orgasms that shook me, passing all the way through to my physical body lying on the floor.

There was hardly time to enjoy this sensation. In the next moment I felt myself quickly expanding, so much so that it exerted tremendous pressure on the edges of my feeling body. Meanwhile my physical body registered the sensation of being fully pregnant and ready — no, bursting to give birth.

Indeed, in the next second a birthing initiated and I saw stars, planets, galaxies, all manner of celestial forms gushing forth from my body. No sooner had the birthing stopped, when I felt that pervading consciousness merging with me again, quaking and shaking me into ecstasy. Again, expanding, becoming enormously pregnant until bursting forth — more planets, more stars, more galaxies, a whole universe.

This continued; the merging, the pregnancy, the birthing — again and again and again. No resting in between. I was exhausted. By this time, I was identifying myself as the Mother of the Omniverse. This is what I felt like. Father seemed to have no other intention than to satisfy his desire.

In my exhaustion, I begged for just a little time to rest; just a little time to breathe in between. My request was not granted. I tried to escape; I tried to move away from the Father, further into the nothingness. As I did, it seemed I would open up more empty space. The Father would catch me, of course, and the next universe we created would go directly into the empty space I had just opened up.

This seemed to go on for hours — I don't know how long. But finally it stopped and we rested.

What I experienced was the separation and reunion of the male and female aspects of Source. The female aspect of Source characterized as the great void, undifferentiated Source, in unity, with no consciousness, just feeling, just movement.

The male aspect of Source being the consciousness — wanting to explore, wanting to know, wanting to understand, wanting to experience. When they merge, consciousness penetrating the void, form is created and birthed.

This was the end of my peak experience that day, but I was left with a knowing of what happened next. The consciousness, or the male aspect of Source, became curious. It awakened to the consciousness of itself and wanted to know who it was.

Because God the Father was holding that question (Who Am I?), the next time he made love to the Mother Goddess, a billion times a billion individualized sparks emerged from Mother Goddess.

One thought intention — "Who Am I" — bursting forth through the birth canal of the Mother, which can be perceived as a Wall of Fire. Source separated and split one consciousness into countless individualized aspects of Mother/Father God.

"You see, when you crossed through the Wall of Fire and experienced separation, you also began to experience "Self" for the first time. You realized you had your own identity and your own spiritual fingerprint.

> There was the realization of Self, but this also created Self-doubt. "Who am I? Why am I here? Why am I no longer at Home? Why am I in a void?" The awareness of Self and Self-doubt also gave you the energy for Self-discovery. You have been on a journey for eons of time, discovering who you are, and who you aren't."
>
> Geoffrey Hoppe, channeling Tobias, www.crimsoncircle.com

The first split of undifferentiated Source was into male and female aspects of God — Male/Female energy. The second split was into these Divine God Sparks of individualized consciousness. Within each Divine God Spark, there were two aspects, one male and one female, Twin Rays, in God's image.

Our individualized consciousness continued to explore itself and experience creation, accumulating perceptions about what is Self and what it is not. Another male/female split occurred that we call Twin Flame.

We traveled further into density, incarnating into bodies. The Oversoul Matrix developed to keep record of our incarnated experiences, exploring creation from inside the limited perception of a body.

We created minds and the emotional body as well as the physical body. Somewhere between the mental body and the emotional body and the role of protecting the identity of Self in physical body, the ego emerged. Again, a split occurred, this time it was between ego-self and the oversoul.

What we call the oversoul created a continuity of soul growth relative to incarnations. The oversoul leads and guides the mind-created ego through many incarnations, playing in density with other members of the soul family. It attempts to bring higher consciousness into the body, breaking down the veil of illusion.

All this is possible now, on this planet, while still in a physical body. We call this ascension, yet this term includes the descension of our Spirit into the body, the ascension of our frequency through ever increasing dimensional doorways and the expansion of our consciousness.

These splits are interpreted by the ego as abandonment and betrayal of Spirit and Source. Since the original emergence from Source, as an individualized Divine Spark, Self has been re-enacting the Illusion of Separation in all of its relationships. In one way or another, we suffer pain in our interactions with others. Even the most loving relationships end in grief when one person dies before the other.

We store the perceptions of separation in our chakra system. We store the dense energies related to separation in our four-body system (physical, mental, emotional and spiritual body). We will continue to re-enact separation, betrayal and abandonment until we break through the veil of illusion and see that there is no separation from Source.

For a *Divine Human*, their inner male and female has released the illusions of separation, resting to a deep space of trust and allowance. The advantage?   Freedom — freedom to create healthy, balanced relationships in the physical world that reflects the healthy balanced state within. Imagine being able to fully open your heart to love, with implicit trust and allowance. Imagine how attractive your undefended heart will be.

Polarity Integration Game

What follows is another initiation that I experienced. Journey along with me this time and remember why we created the Polarity Integration Game.

Find yourself in front of a platinum archway. As you stand looking through it, you see a room with no ceiling or floor and no walls - you are looking into a black hole, an expansive void. As you search with your eyes - begin to see in the distance a glimmer, a sparkle of stars, and now you find that your feet are leaving the ground as you float slowly through the archway and out into the galaxy.

You are traveling through this velvet black, and you are enveloped with a sense of peace, of calm, you are swimming in contentment. You can feel your body and at the same time, you don't feel connected to it as you continue to travel towards the sparkle and glimmer of distant stars.

Feel the peace of this nothingness. Hear the silence. Know that you are at one with this void. This void is you.

Now as you approach the glimmer, getting closer and closer, the stars seem to multiply, more and more stars appear, you see a galaxy moving in a whirling vortex, spiraling to it's center.

You move with the energy of these stars - pulled by the vortex into the center. In the center - you find a beautiful pillar of light. It is a blend of ruby red and pure white light dancing in *Sacred Union* - and you become aware, you know, that this same pillar of light enfolds and fills your physical body as it rests in a sphere of compassion far, far below us...

Now enter this pillar of light and feel yourself drawn upward, higher and higher, picking up speed, moving faster and faster. Feel the energy building, the intensity increasing, the light is brilliant, almost blinding. Continue upwards until you begin to know that you have come to the heart of Source - the center of the great central sun, the father God, Source of all that is ... feel yourself embraced, enfolded, filled with this powerful energy.

You are now home, and you are so loved, and you are so cherished, and you are so treasured.

Know this, feel this, revel in this pure power, this pure love, this pure light. As you are embraced, you embrace the light in return and in this embrace, feel and know that you are dissolving, you are blending, you are merging and becoming one with the Source of All That Is.

Now you are Divine energy and you are one with Source. Undifferentiated Source. Pure energy, pure light. The consciousness of allness, and oneness and nothingness. Before consciousness. Then there is a movement, a stirring.

Who am I that feels like the Mother? Who am I that desires the Mother and wants to make love with her? Who are we that created those heavenly bodies? Who are we as these heavenly bodies? What is our relationship to each other?

Integrating Polarity

The question, "Who Am I?" sends out trillions of Divine Sparks to answer this question. Feel yourself now as one of these Divine Sparks. A consciousness made of the Mother and Father, part of the Mother and Father, one with the Mother and Father and yet now, individualized consciousness, feeling separate and yet one at the same time. Seeking the answer to Mother/Father God's questions; all exploring this question in your own unique way; expressing your answers in your own unique way based on your individualized experience.

So we, as Divine Sparks, emerge from Mother/Father God in waves, a wave of Archangels, then the Archangels splitting themselves again, individualized their consciousness further into more aspects of themselves, creating the angelic realm.

From another wave, simultaneously emerges the original 12 Creator Gods. Then splitting themselves, creating aspects of themselves, setting the intention for each aspect to explore a different particular part of creation. These Creator Gods and Angels working together now, creating together, joyously experimenting, playing, learning, reporting back to Mother/Father God everything they learn. Creator Gods and Angels loving each other, merging together, creating new beings, splitting their consciousness into more finite aspects, setting the intention to explore creation in new and more creative ways.

All the while, you as that original Divine Spark have now split yourselves many times to experience creation in different ways and different places. Joyously delighting in EXPERIENCE. Experience is celebrated. Experience is the delicious candy of creation. Experience is the gift of individualized consciousness. Each aspect of you reporting back to your experience to your original Divine Spark, and reporting back to Mother/Father God. All Divine Sparks doing the same thing.

We see from this play and exploration, there begins to emerge games with rules of order. The games evolve and become more sophisticated. And the Creator Gods begin to specialize. Some specialize as game engineers, setting up the games, creating the rules of the game, creating the game board so to speak on a planet. Some creator gods and goddesses specialize as genetic engineers, working with the DNA, creating all sorts of beings to inhabit the planets — plants, animals and sentient creatures.

Some beings on some planets might look like humanoids. Other beings on other planets may look feline or reptilian, cetaceans like dolphins or whales. Some are crystalline. Some never have dense bodies — just light bodies. A huge variety of forms.

There are other Creator Gods who specialize in creating the energy grids around the planets — creating and maintaining portals and star gates and vortexes. We see that when a new universe is discovered, a team of experts is called in to populate it. A game is decided on and then game engineers begin their job setting up the game board and the rules of order — the creation myth and the underlying belief systems that will keep the game in order. The genetic engineers begin creating life and the energy engineers create the energy grids to support the life and the game. All of the experts are working together to create a new game in a new universe.

Come back now to your awareness of you as a Divine Spark. See that you have created many aspects of yourself, which you might look on as your own children. See that they have merged with other aspects of other Divine Sparks and created grandchildren. But you can trace your lineage. Your energetic signature is distinct. You can see all aspects of yourself wherever they are in creation. They are all connected.

Now let's explore the universe where Earth is. Back before there was life there. Before it was populated and was still just a celestial body. This universe was discovered and the decision was made that in this universe the Creator Gods would play the Polarity Integration Game. This is the most evolved and sophisticated game. It is a rich and sensual game. It is an exciting game with plenty of risk and drama. It is game that affords much learning and growth and insight. Lots of experience can happen in this game. Remember, we love EXPERIENCE.

So you, in one of your aspects might have been aware of this universe, of this sector of the universe where Earth is. Maybe not. Maybe your awareness, your attention wasn't focused here until later. Maybe like me, you were involved in many aspects of its setup. A certain aspect participating as a genetic engineer, another aspect as a game engineer, another aspect on the team that set up and maintained the energy.

Watch now, because if you didn't participate in the creation of this particular planet, you were out in the cosmos working on another. Remember again when you were still part of undifferentiated Source. Remember that sacred question that began it all. Who Am I? Remember your first realization as a Divine Spark, of an individualized consciousness who would answer that question through experience.

Place your awareness with one or more of the aspects of you, as a collective, a team, setting up the polarity Integration Game on Earth. In this game you begin creating the opposite poles, which are the foundation of the game.

Allow yourself to be in that consciousness of a Creator God/Goddess, remember with me what it was like. Imagine you command, "I create the Day and the Night. I bring forth the Good and the Evil. I make the Separation and the Union. I form Commitment and I form Betrayal. I create Abandonment and Connection. I invent Anger and Love. I create Fear and Joy. I make the Yin and the Yang. I form the Masculine and the Feminine. I bring forth the Ego and the Spirit. I create the Physical and the Divine. I manifest the polarities, the polar opposites and all variations in between."

Then as your Divine Spark Consciousness you look at aspects of yourself creating scenarios, like movies to play in this game. You are giving the command to create the villains and the heroes, the damsel in distress. Just like in the movies, there are only nine distinct plotlines, and all stories are like movies, just variations on the theme. But the movies are rich and sensual and diverse, they promise to evoke all manner of experience. All of these stories are downloaded into the grid work around the planet.

Embrace this feeling of creation and celebration and accomplishment. Feel the celebration at this Divine Plan. Feel the sense of oneness with Source with your Divine Spark consciousness. Feel the oneness with other aspects of yourself and the oneness with other Divine Sparks and their family of aspects. All of this experience of creation is exhilarating and joyous. Up until now you have felt this experience from your spirit consciousness.

Your Divine Spark consciousness decides to go one level deeper into creation to experience life within the world of form; to take on the mantle of human form; to experience the body and its rich sensations, to experience emotions. You know that to fully enter into the game, you must believe that it is real. You must forget that it is a game. That's the only way to fully experience this type of creation. So you take away your own memory of Who You Really Are. You create the veil of forgetfulness. You create the Illusion of Separation. And you choose the roles you want to play.

You have heard often that time is also an illusion. Imagine with me; remember with me that Now moment when we were all getting ready to breathe ourselves into form. We were deciding what roles we wanted to play in which movies. Oh, there was much excitement. We had our favorite spirit friends and aspects of ourselves. We choose the family of souls to play with in many movies. You be the villain this time, and I will be next time. You abandon me, I'll betrayal you. Sometimes we'll be lovers, sometimes friends, sometimes enemies. Mother, father, sister, teacher. Look at the creativity.

The basic premise of the Polarity Integration Game is that you EXPERIENCE the extreme polarities. Blocks, obstacles are created to make experience more and more challenging as we go along. Illusions are created. Lies are told, situations manipulated. Can you move through the illusions without being pulled off center? That is a challenge. Can you discern the truth in the face of all the illusion? That is a challenge. Of course, we anticipate the fulfilling feeling when we overcome an obstacle or meet a challenge. It's all part of the game.

Look at the excitement as we discussed these things. Some of us follow a very focused systematic plan for our exploration of experience within this game. Some of us are preparing to just go and play with no apparent focus.

Integrating Polarity

Now looking at this game board we call Earth. All this experience is being played out simultaneously, but in different dimensions. And we want to experience it all. So we create the illusion of time. We create the mind as a tool, imprinted with the illusion of time. The mind slows down the awareness that is moving through your consciousness. It slows it down so it can look at it by frame, like slowing it down a film. It slows it down so you can make connections between cause and effect, so you can learn. And yet the mind operates within the illusions of the game. Its perceptions are colored by the made up rules and illusions of the game. And we agree to this plan. You helped create this plan.

See, feel and know that this creation - this Polarity Integration Game is good and rich and vibrant and vital and alive. You are well pleased. Feel the sense of accomplishment and excitement at this Divine Plan that you have participated in creating.

Now send yourself, breathe yourself into the game. Take some long deep breaths and sending aspects of yourself into many different bodies in many different dimensions surrounding Earth. Breath yourself into life within the game. If you've seen the movie Matrix, they depicted this transition of bringing your awareness into a body within the game matrix. It is much like that.

In your Divine Spark Consciousness, overlook all of the Earth incarnations, as well as other aspects of you experiencing life in other dimensions around other planets in other universes. See that all incarnations of you, from your Divine Spark are connected and passing information between each other in your unconscious awareness. The joys and fears of one are transmitted to others at an unconscious level.

Now imagine that all aspects of you are invited into your Time Space Continuum. Your Divine Spark self calls a meeting and you all show up. All aspects of you, in all time, all dimensions, in the golden tunnel. Discussions are happening and the most common experience that everyone is talking about is how easy it is to get pulled off center and out of balance when you are in a dense body. You talk about how real the Illusion of Separation feels when you are in body. How much you feel a lack of connection, it feels like an emptiness, a hole you want to fill. You talk about how all of you experience a sense of longing to fill that hole, to come to completeness. You can see a black hole near the heart of each aspect of yourself. You talk about how easy it is to be pulled into addictive, compulsive and obsessive behaviors in an effort to fill that void. In your discussions, it becomes clear to all of you, how and why you've passed this feeling of incompleteness back and forth to each other, unconsciously reinforcing it; all manifesting it and experiencing it in a myriad of unique ways.

You see aspects of yourself, in the tunnel, that represent the extreme polar opposites – the angels and the demons. You see all of the variations in between the extremes. You see the Veil of Forgetfulness and the Illusion of Separation. Now you make a decision. It is a collective decision, including all aspects of yourself in all dimensions, with the support of your Divine Spark consciousness. You decide that you are complete with the Polarity Integration Game.

You are satisfied, and complete with the richness of experience and drama that polarity afforded you. You are satisfied and complete with the lessons you learned, the wisdom and knowledge you have accumulated and shared with Mother/Father God/Goddess and undifferentiated Source. Feel the gratitude for these experiences.

No you can choose to command integration. By embracing the polarities, by integrating them, by loving them, we bring them into balance and into wholeness. Make this command.

I AM the Day and the Night. I AM the Good and the Evil. I AM Separation and Union. I AM Commitment and Betrayal. I AM Abandonment and Connection. I AM Anger and Joy. I AM Fear and Love. I AM the Masculine and the Feminine. I AM the Child and the Adult. I AM Ego and Spirit. I AM the Yin and the Yang. I AM Physical and Divine. I AM All That Is. I AM That I Am.

I now command: every lifetime, experience, history or story, known and unknown, remembered or forgotten, in all times, all realities, all dimensions, all universes and all levels of consciousness. To release and surrender, to balance and heal, all patterns of lack and limitation, all illusions of separation and incompleteness, all feelings of inadequacy, and all addictions, compulsions and obsessions. I Am balance. I Am integration union. I am harmony. I am the dance of creation. I am *Sacred Union* of all polarities. I AM THAT I AM.

Now bring your attention to that black hole near the heart center of all aspects of you. This black hole is the void. It has been misinterpreted. It is the way you are connected to the Supreme Mother of All That Is. In our misinterpretation we have been trying to fill it, instead of allowing it to fill us. So let's call upon the Supreme Mother now. Let's call her in to fill us with her Divine Mother energy.

Feel the Supreme Mothers energy enter through that hole, pouring into all aspects of yourself, including the aspect of your current lifetime. Fill yourself to overflowing with the Supreme Mother energy. Recognize the Platinum Ray and it feels like pure joy, pure bliss and pure ecstasy all in one.

Thank your Divine Spark consciousness and all aspects of yourself for showing up in your time/space continuum today. Allow yourself to feel their gratitude for the leadership you have shown. Lovingly dismiss them from the tunnel. Anchor the energy of balance, wholeness and completeness — *Sacred Union* into your body and then into the Earth. You are an acupuncture needle in the earth for integration, balance, wholeness and completeness.

Installation Command

If you choose to activate this initiation, give this command:

I AM That I AM. I AM That I AM. I AM That I AM. I now command the activation of the *Divine Human Upgrade* called *Integrating Polarity*. I open my heart and command all levels of my consciousness to fully receive the gifts of this upgrade. I command my outer self to allow and embrace the needed lessons and changes this upgrade brings into my life now. I command easy, comfortable, graceful and joyful integration of the new features, higher frequencies and expanded consciousness delivered through this upgrade. So Be It. So It Is.

Integration

Integration of this upgrade will be similar to the others. You will continue to become aware of old programming that no longer serves you as a *Divine Human*. Continue with the same Integration Exercises:

- Journaling
- Apple cider vinegar baths
- Integration Meditation
- Releasing What No Longer Serves You

What does polarity integration mean for your life? It means that since you have integrated the polarities, you can no longer be pulled off center. You fee whole and complete. There are no holes to fill and you easily let go of addictions, obsessions and compulsions. You can feel free to enjoy life, in balance, in moderation, in harmony. You no longer believe in the illusions of this world. You see only the truth. It is easy for you to be discerning. You choose to only give your precious attention to that which you would like to create for your own enjoyment and amusement. Your karmic lessons are over. Your karmic debts are released. You can spend each moment in the balance of Divine Love, Divine Power and Divine Wisdom. You are free to begin creating your version of Paradise on Earth. You are now prepared to receive your own I AM presence into your body as a purified bride would receive her bridegroom.

Using the New Features

When you integrate polarity, you will no longer judge things as good or bad, black or white, up or down. Compassion becomes your friend, not only your best personal friend, but a friend you naturally want to share with everyone else.

There is a deepening of the realization that it is perfect to let everyone else play the games they want to play. There is a deepening of your dedication to being in integrity with your own Divine Plan. Your discernment skills deepen as does your ability to speak the truth from your heart with respect.

You let go of the belief that you have to see everything balance out in your life. Many of us believe that you can only have so much good, before something bad happens. You are always waiting for the other shoe to drop. You think that our joy has to be balanced by sorrow. You believe you can only appreciate joy if you also feel the sorrow. You've had enough sorrow-filled lifetimes. You know it well. You can choose joy in every moment. Of course maybe you will get bored with it and need to create sorrow to spice things up. It's all up to you now. In the fifth dimension, the denser emotional frequencies of anger, sorrow, grief and pain will not be in our reality. Are you ready to let them go?

Divine Birth

Upgrade Description

In the Divine Birth upgrade, we bring your God/Goddess Cell right into your sacrum. This is your creative source engine. It is an energy battery from your Divine Spark. We reprogram the mind to align itself with your *Divine Plan* so that it will work in cooperation (*Sacred Union*) with your Plan and God/Goddess Cell to manifest everything needed to fulfill your Blueprint with passion, joy, comfort and beauty.

We connect, activate, ignite and ground in the physical body the 12-Strand *Divine Human* DNA. We re-write the script for your life, starting before you were conceived; giving you a new set of emotional and mental memories of growing up with *Divine Human* parents who loved you unconditionally, encouraged you to express your authentic self and taught you how to use the gifts of the 12 Strands of DNA.

Going back to the computer metaphor, this effectively installs a brand new operating system. You are now a newborn Divine Child free to explore a new world: Life on Earth in the fifth dimension.

Our guide for this upgrade is the Council of Creation. This Council is a collection of spiritual beings that sponsor this Divine Birth project. They gifted us with this spiritual technology. We invite them to implement your Divine Birth. They will work with us, rewriting your records and hooking up and activating your DNA.

Now also call forward your Advisor of Integrity. Remember, this advisor was formally the deva of the subprogram of the mind that was in charge of creating and maintaining your Earth identity that most refer to as ego. In an earlier initiation we uninstalled the mind-created identity (ego) and installed your Divine Human identity, an upgrade that the Advisor of Integrity has been following since that time.

It's now time to do some last minute house cleaning of some of the more self-destructive programming that you carried with you from before you first incarnated into a human body. You have chosen this lifetime for final release.

We will ask the Advisor of Integrity to find and uninstall programming that is no longer consistent with our Divine Identity and our Divine Plan, including: separation, self-hatred, self-loathing, self-sabotage and self-destruction programs, strategies and data files.

We uninstall addictions, attachments, obsessions, compulsions, anything that overrides your ability to honor your Divine Plan in each now moment. We get rid of curses, hexes and spells, control devices, scrambling devices, implants, entities, miasmas and energies not in alignment with your Divine Human Blueprint in a joy-based reality. We let go of all contracts, vows and agreements not in alignment with your Divine Plan in a joy-based reality.

We install, activate and ignite Divine Body Blueprint that is impervious to aging and illness.

We install Divine Intelligence. Remember, the mind is a very sophisticated artificial intelligence software program. We call it artificial intelligence because it "learns" by observing cause/effect relationships and patterns and creating new rules based on those observations. These new rules are then used as a basis for subsequent manifestation in the physical world. We honor the mind for the excellent job it has been doing for us.

But now, we are ready to receive the ultimate upgrade. In fact, it is a whole new operating system we call Divine Intelligence. This new operating system includes many of the processing capabilities of the mind, but is expanded to go far beyond that. The new operating system does not learn — it knows. Divine Intelligence is the knowingness of All That Is.

This new operating system will give you the ability to translate multi-dimensional information in ways you cannot even imagine right now. The result in your life, will be that in every NOW moment of your life, you will KNOW, with absolute certainty, whatever you need to KNOW to express yourself as a Divine Human, operating in a joy-based reality, creating your version of Paradise on Earth.

Divine Birth

The Advisor of Integrity still has the same job of advising you how to keep in alignment with your Divine Human master blueprint. Now it will have access and be able to translate information coming in from multi-dimensional levels. Even though you will have access to much more KNOWING, it will not be overwhelming. The Advisor of Integrity will advise you on what action is needed in every NOW moment. You will have just enough guidance and just enough energy to take the right action in every moment.

We install your God Cell. It is like a battery of Source energy that will fuel your creations in this physical world. Your I AM Presence will install this God Cell right into your sacrum.

How do these new gifts work together? Your Divine Intelligence, which resides in and around your body, will be receiving information and frequencies that will continue to move you through this transformation from "only human" to "Divine Human." Your Advisor of Integrity will be reading the information, frequencies, your Divine Plan and advise you how to direct your energy in each NOW moment. Your God Cell will be fueling your desires and creations; attracting to you all the resources necessary to express yourself in joy as a Divine Human Creator God/Goddess creating Paradise on Earth.

After installing the New Operating System, you need to a new set of default data files. We rewrite your history. This new history includes an upgraded version of your parents as transformed Divine Humans, with 12 strands of DNA. They raise you in unconditional love, fully knowing Who You Really Are, what your Divine Plan is, encouraging you to develop and express your unique gifts and talents in accordance with your Divine Plan. As you are growing, they teach you how to use the wonderful abilities that come along with being a being with 12 strands of DNA.

When the Council of Creation gave me the instructions to "rewrite the script" for Divine Parents raising Divine Humans, I had no idea how. There is no written blueprint for that on this planet. I had to travel multi-dimensionally to find a model. I believe I found the blueprint in Shambhalla where the Ascended Masters hang out.

So as you move through this upgrade, we rewrite the history in your DNA; also known as your Akashic Records. We write a new story and anchor the emotions of love, joy and gratitude to these new memories. This is how we create a new reality. This is what makes it feel real to you. Here is the blueprint for raising a Divine Human.

Birth to 4 Years

Looking at that time between your Divine Birth and 4 years of age: your parents have created a very safe and child-friendly environment where you are totally free to explore. They are encouraging you to freely express yourself. They are teaching you how to speak the truth, from your heart, with respect. They honor and respect all that you say and reward you for speaking your truth, even when it is uncomfortable or inconvenient for them to hear.

They are teaching you how to communicate with all beings in nature, in spirit, and the consciousness that is in all form. It's a magical time. Everything in the world is alive, communicating with you and loving you. You feel completely loved and safe to express yourself in this new world of form.

4 to 8 years

Your parents are teaching how to listen and communicate with your body so it tells you what it needs in terms of proper nutrition, rest, exercise and joyful expression. Your parents respect and honor these communications from your body and you are learning how to nourish yourself with the support of your parents and Mother Earth.

Your parents teach you how to tune into your energy field and monitor it and keep it balanced, flowing and healthy. Feel yourself being nourished energetically by Mother Earth and the Source of All That Is. The whole family enjoys talking about their dreams every morning. These dreams are discussed and honored for their guidance value and for how they help to integrate your life experiences.

8 to 12 years

During this time, you are discovering and beginning to express your talents. You have developed a strong spiritual presence. Your parents demonstrate their value and recognition of who you really are. You are encouraged to express yourself creatively. Your spiritual and physical vitality is celebrated. Your parents are teaching you various techniques to go within and contact your Inner Advisors for guidance. They respect and honor the guidance you bring forth.

12 to 16 years

You are moving through puberty and adolescence. You are getting in touch with your gender identity and sexuality. Your parents have modeled free and appropriate expression of their love and sexuality. You begin to explore your own body and begin to be interested in other types of bodies. Sexual exploration is free and easy; a normal, expected part of the growing up process. By now you have strengthened your senses and intuition to the point that you have a keen sense of discernment, integrity and self-responsibility. So you attract friends — playmates of the same high integrity.

Your parents have modeled *Sacred Union*. They are both balanced in their male/female energy. They honor the both the male and female expressions of energy in each other and in their relationship.

Both parents model beings that are expressing themselves freely in the world. They prioritize their decisions and actions by valuing the heart over the mind. They model a meditative-type life style, where most of the time you are in an open, receptive being state, free of thought. You are open to inspiration and communication from all of life at all times. You use your mind to plan and carry out tasks. And when the tasks are complete, you relax back in to the receptive being state.

16 to 20 years

Between your 16th and 20th years, you are beginning to explore your identity in relationship to the world. Based on your talents and life's purpose, you are beginning to prepare for further education, or possibly an apprenticeship or self-directed or spirit-directed course of study.

You find that your parents are completely supportive in helping you move along the Golden Path that you have set for yourself. They teach you how to manifest, using your creative mind and energy. They teach you to attract all that you desire to carry out your Divine Plan and enjoy your life in beauty and comfort.

21 years old

Your feet are walking with confidence and joy along your Golden Path. Your parents are still available for support and guidance, but you are enjoying your freedom and spreading your wings. You are manifesting abundance. You know your life's purpose and are aligned with it. Your male and female aspects are completely balanced and working together in *Sacred Union* within you. You are overflowing with love and joy. You are a Divine Human in full power.

If in your past fear-based life, you had addictions or compulsive thoughts or behaviors, you see these lose their control over you. You see that there is no way that you will slip back into the fear-based reality. You are having too much fun in your joy-based reality, which is getting stronger and stronger everyday.

Installation Command

If you choose to activate this initiation, give this command:

I AM That I AM. I AM That I AM. I AM That I AM. I now command the activation of the *Divine Human Upgrade* called *Divine Birth*. I open my heart and command all levels of my consciousness to fully receive the gifts of this upgrade. I command my outer self to allow and embrace the needed lessons and changes this upgrade brings into my life now. I command easy, comfortable, graceful and joyful integration of the new features, higher frequencies and expanded consciousness delivered through this upgrade. So Be It. So It Is.

Integration

Integration of this upgrade will be similar to the others. You will continue to become aware of old programming that no longer serves you as a *Divine Human*. Continue with the same Integration Exercises:

- Journaling
- Apple cider vinegar baths
- Integration Meditation
- Releasing What No Longer Serves You

This transformation moment to moment is very subtle and every once in a while you notice how you are making different choices. You are reacting differently, more open-heartedly, more joyfully, without judgment. You are speaking your truth from your heart with respect. Everyday the new hologram that is your reality is shifting more and more to be in alignment with the change in the Akashic Records and DNA.

You notice that your Advisor of the Divine Body is speaking to you loudly and clearly now about what it needs for its proper nourishment, healing, balance and energy flow. Your Advisor is bringing you creative opportunities to move your body into alignment with the Divine Body Blueprint. You many notice that your taste buds and food preferences have changed. You may notice interest awakening in different forms of music and creative expression.

You notice that both your inner male and female are balanced, mature and working together in *Sacred Union*. You spend more and more time in an open and receptive state of no thought. In this receptive, feminine state inspiration comes to you easily. All of nature and spirit communicates with you. Once inspired, you use your masculine mind to carry out the tasks that inspired you. Your masculine side knows how to ground spirit into form. For example, your feminine side may come up with an idea on a new business venture or creative project and then your masculine side may do the research and make the contacts necessary to put the idea into action.

Everyday, in every way, you are shifting, releasing and inviting more and more joy into your life. Relationships and situations that no longer resonate with you as a Divine Human are falling away easily and gracefully. New people and opportunities that resonate with your new vibration are showing up for your enjoyment.

You are finding that subconscious thought patterns that used to run in the background are coming up into your consciousness for release. When they show up, you determine their usefulness to you. And if they do not serve you as a Divine Human, you command their release and let them go with the piston breath.

Using the New Features

This upgrade in particular is the central point of the whole series. I highly recommend that you experience this live via a private session or teleclass AND purchase the CD recording. Since we are installing the new operating system and rewriting the default programming, this one needs more conscious reinforcement than the rest.

That said, the new feature that is the by product of this upgrade is Self-Love. Love is not something we do, it is what we are. As you have been progressing through these upgrades, you have let go of the self-sabotage programming that made it feel unsafe to be totally in your body with an open heart.

As you feel safe to open your heart, more love will flow through you until you are an overflowing fountain of love, joyfully splashing on to everyone who comes near. Your dedication to staying in integrity with your Divine Plan will lead you to make decisions that are more self-nurturing and self-nourishing. You will stop judging yourself. And the self love begins to grow.

This has a lot to do with the new history you have installed. When growing up with Divine Human parents who showered you with unconditional love, didn't have their own wounds to project on to you, and encouraged you do express your Divinity — well you would love yourself, wouldn't you? So the practice here is to allow yourself to make those self-nourishing, self-nurturing decisions.

Divine Birth

Again, you may notice another set of changes in your relationships, because you have made another quantum leap in frequency and consciousness. As you practice nurturing yourself, you will notice that others will mirror this respect back to you. You will attract new friends and associates who respect and love themselves.

Clear and compassionate communication is easier as you attract other Divine Humans to you. You will notice a huge difference when you surround yourself with people who take conscious responsibility for creating their own reality.

Twin Flame Completion

Upgrade Description

After integrating the Divine Birth for a while, you are ready to merge with your Twin Flame. Your Twin Flame is a part of you that holds the energy of the opposite gender expression. Usually our Twin Flame is in spirit when we are embodied.

The journey to *Sacred Union* Consciousness is all about integrating male and female expressions of energy at all levels. Let's reflect on how this has been true in the previous upgrades. First you integrated the male/female expressions of your personality, then you integrated the mental (male) and emotional (female) aspects of yourself. The *Sacred Union* of the Divine Mind (male) with the physical Mother Earth (female).

This process of *Sacred Union* of male and female expressions continues. Before you incarnated onto this Earth Plane, you split into a male and female expressions called Twin Flames. You have done this many, many times, in each dimension of creation.

The first split was your emergence as a Divine Spark. You emerged as an individualized consciousness (male) from the void (female) of All That Is. Then as a Divine Spark, you split again into male/female aspects called Twin Rays.

In this upgrade, you merge with your Twin Flame who is the next highest level to you in human form. You set up a pathway of light, so that as you integrate one level, the next higher level descends into your body for *Sacred Union*. This process will continue until Twin Ray Completion.

To consciously acknowledge and merge with your Twin Flame is an awesome experience. In many cases it is the illusionary separation of yourself that has led you to long for a partner to complete you. Many clients report finally feeling whole and complete. The desperate need and longing to find a mate recedes and you find you want to begin a romance with yourself.

In this beautiful upgrade, you journey to two temples. The first one is the wedding temple where you experience an incredibly beautiful and nurturing purification and beautification ritual to prepare you for your wedding to your Twin Flame. Then the wedding ceremony is preformed with much pomp and circumstance in the company of many jubilant spiritual celebrants gathered at the temple to honor you.

Once merged in *Sacred Union* with your Twin Flame you can go to the Ascension Temple of Serapis Bey and appear before the Ascension Tribunal and ask for your ascension. If the Tribunal sees that you are ready, you will be granted your ascension. You don't have to leave the body to do this. After integration and mastery of this level of ascension, you can truly be called an Ascended Master walking upon the Earth.

At your ascension you merge with Source and create a path of light for the higher male/female aspects to follow back to your body as you are ready to integrate them.

As each successive level of your higher dimensional selves merge into your body in the coming months and years, they bring with them wisdom, skills and knowledge from their multi-dimensional experience.

Installation Command

If you choose to activate this initiation, give this command:

I AM That I AM. I AM That I AM. I AM That I AM. I now command the activation of the *Divine Human Upgrade* called *Twin Flame Completion*. I open my heart and command all levels of my consciousness to fully receive the gifts of this upgrade. I command my outer self to allow and embrace the needed lessons and changes this upgrade brings into my life now. I command easy, comfortable, graceful and joyful integration of the new features, higher frequencies and expanded consciousness delivered through this upgrade. So Be It. So It Is.

Integration

Integration of this upgrade will be similar to the others. You will continue to become aware of old programming that no longer serves you as a *Divine Human*. Continue with the same Integration Exercises:

- Journaling
- Apple cider vinegar baths
- Integration Meditation
- Releasing What No Longer Serves You

This is a time to romance yourself. Write a list of the most romantic things you would like a partner to do, and do these for yourself. If you are planning on calling a *Sacred Union Partner* into your life, or elevating your current relationship to *Sacred Union* status, you need to get grounded in what a *Sacred Union Relationship* means to you.

This is a self-exploration. It is a time to get to know what you want, what is nourishing to you, what your boundaries are and what you want to give. When you know this about yourself, then you can more effectively communicate this to a partner.

Using the New Features

As you feel inspired, call for *Sacred Union* at the next highest level. You can use the Twin Flame Completion CD to call in the male/female pairs at the next higher level of your being. Make it a Sacred Ceremony. Remember to command that the integration be graceful.

If there are personal characteristics, qualities, wisdom, knowledge and skills that you would like to express, you may ask that higher levels of your being merge and bring you these qualities. You can follow the same technique as downloading a program, making it a bit more sacred to honor these higher aspects of yourself.

For example, I called in an aspect of me that I had heard about during a past-life reading. This aspect sits on the Council of Orion as a mediator between Light and Dark. I knew that this aspect of me was honored for the skill of razor-sharp discernment and compassion. I had been feeling a need to improve my discernment skills. I created a sacred ceremony and invited this aspect of me to merge in *Sacred Union* with my body.

I knew it worked when only a few days later I was asked to attend a ho'oponopono (Hawaiian mediation ritual) for a couple of friends of mine. I had never received a request like this before. I was told by the requestor, that he asked Spirit, in his meditation, for an appropriate ho'oponopono partner and was given my name. He had made the same request weeks before I merged with my higher aspect, and no name came to him. This was wonderful validation that the process works. You will receive validation on your efforts every step of the way. Especially if you ask for it.

The New You

Twelve Signs of Your Awakening Divinity

Reprinted with permission by Geoffrey Hoppe and Tobias. http://www.crimsoncircle.com   Note: The word "Shaumbra" is Tobias's term for *Divine Human*.

1. **Body aches and pains, especially in the neck, shoulder and back.** This is the result of intense changes at your DNA level as the "Christ seed" awakens within. This too shall pass.

2. **Feeling of deep inner sadness for no apparent reason.** You are releasing your past (this lifetime and others) and this causes the feeling of sadness. This is similar to the experience of moving from a house where you lived for many, many years into a new house. As much as you want to move into the new house, there is a sadness of leaving behind the memories, energy and experiences of the old house. This too shall pass.

3. **Crying for no apparent reason.** Similar to #2 above. It's good and healthy to let the tears flow. It helps to release the old energy within. This too shall pass.

4. **Sudden change in job or career.** A very common symptom. As you change, things around you will change as well. Don't worry about finding the "perfect" job or career right now. This too shall pass. You're in transition and you may make several job changes before you settle into one that fits your passion.

5. **Withdrawal from family relationships.** You are connected to your biological family via old karma. When you get off the karmic cycle, the bonds of the old relationships are released. It will appear as though you are drifting away from your family and friends. This too shall pass. After a period of time, you may develop a new relationship with them if it is appropriate. However, the relationship will be based in the new energy without the karmic attachments.

6. **Unusual sleep patterns.** It's likely that you'll awaken many nights between 2:00 and 4:00 AM. There's a lot of work going on within you, and it often causes you to wake up for a

"breather." Not to worry. If you can't go back to sleep, get up and do something rather than lie in bed and worry about humanly things. This too shall pass.

7. **Intense dreams.** These might include war and battle dreams, chase dreams or monster dreams. You are literally releasing the old energy within, and these energies of the past are often symbolized as wars, running to escape and boogiemen. This too shall pass.

8. **Physical disorientation.** At times you'll feel very ungrounded. You'll be "spatially challenged" with feeling like you can't put two feet on the ground, or that you're walking between two worlds. As your consciousness transitions into the new energy, your body sometimes lags behind. Spend more time in nature to help ground the new energy within. This too shall pass.

9. **Increased "self talk."** You'll find yourself talking to your Self more often. You'll suddenly realize you've been chattering away with yourself for the past 30 minutes. There is a new level of communication taking place within your being, and you're experiencing the tip of the iceberg with the self talk. The conversations will increase, and they will become more fluid, more coherent and more insightful. You're not going crazy; you're just Shaumbra moving into the new energy.

10. **Feelings of loneliness, even when in the company of others.** You may feel alone and removed from others. You may feel the desire to "flee" groups and crowds. As Shaumbra, you are walking a sacred and lonely path. As much as the feelings of loneliness cause you anxiety, it is difficult to relate to others at this time. The feelings of loneliness are also associated with the fact that your Guides have departed. They have been with you on all of your journeys in all of your lifetimes. It was time for them to back away so you could fill your space with your own divinity. This too shall pass. The void within will be filled with the love and energy of your own Christ consciousness.

11. **Loss of passion.** You may feel totally disimpassioned, with little or no desire to do anything. That's okay, and it's just part of the process. Take this time to "do no-thing." Don't fight yourself on this, because this too shall pass. It's similar to

rebooting a computer. You need to shut down for a brief period of time in order to load the sophisticated new software, or in this case, the new Christ-seed energy.

12. **A deep longing to go Home**. This is perhaps the most difficult and challenging of any of the conditions. You may experience a deep and overwhelming desire to leave the planet and return to Home. This is not a "suicidal" feeling. It is not based in anger or frustration. You don't want to make a big deal of it or cause drama for yourself or others. There is a quiet part of you that wants to go Home. The root cause for this is quite simple. You have completed your karmic cycles. You have completed your contract for this lifetime. You are ready to begin a new lifetime while still in this physical body. During this transition process, you have an inner remembrance of what it is like to be on the other side. Are you ready to enlist for another tour of duty here on Earth? Are you ready to take on the challenges of moving into the New Energy? Yes, indeed you could go Home right now. But you've come this far, and after many, many lifetimes it would be a shame to leave before the end of the movie. Besides, Spirit needs you here to help others transition into the new energy. They will need a human guide, just like you, who has taken the journey from the old energy into the new. The path you're walking right now provides the experiences to enable you to become a Teacher of the New *Divine Human*. As lonely and dark as your journey can be at times, remember that you are never alone.

Divine Humanity

Starting as a new-born Divine Child, you will grow up quickly and walk swiftly into the shoes of an Ascended Master. There will be a period of practice until Mastery. There are few anywhere, even those you have called your Ascended Master teachers, who can tell you how to walk this walk — so new it is in all of Creation.

The keyword is Mastery: mastery of your energy, mastery of your mind, mastery of your emotions, mastery of your body and mastery of illusion. Bring your full master presence into each moment. Bring your open heart, which floods the world with compassion, fully into each moment. Your body is an acupuncture needle in the Earth for the higher frequencies of light. Just walking around, being who you are, is your service. Express yourself creatively in whatever way brings you joy. When you are in joy, your capacity to flow light through you expands. It doesn't really matter what activity your body or mind is engaged in. If you are in joy, then the light flows through you and radiates out in all directions.

When I say it doesn't matter what you do, I don't mean do nothing. Quite the contrary. Being a *Divine Human* will probably keep you very busy. But that busyness (business) won't feel like work because you are expressing yourself creatively.

Start right now, wherever you are. You don't have to quit your job. You don't have to quit your relationship. Bring your mastery into the job fully. If you are present in full love and joy, expressing yourself creatively, the job or the relationship will either transform to match you or a new opportunity will be presented to you. Master your current situation, transmute it and then see what creation offers you next.

Here's a practical example. When I was in the corporate world, I delivered business training within the auto industry. I knew that my purpose on Earth wasn't to teach guys how to sell more cars. At the same time, I knew that I was developing skills and confidence in my teaching abilities. In one of my last assignments that lasted about five months, each week a new group of 40 men would arrive for training. How could I make the most of it? How could I express myself creatively? How could I live my passion (which is ascension) when I was teaching business process and computer upgrades?

After some meditation, I was inspired to set up an energy grid in the classroom, surrounding it with an energetic sphere of compassion, programmed to activate all who were ready, into their ascension process. Every Sunday night before the next new batch of students arrived, I would connect with them in their hearts and talk to their Higher Selves. I would let them know about the ascension opportunities that were available to them. Then their Higher Selves either guided them to partake of the energies or not.

The New You

A funny thing started to happen. We were training the western region reps in Scottsdale, Arizona. The eastern region reps were being trained in Detroit, Michigan. All reps were receiving the same curriculum. The reps in the western region enjoyed their training week and had a good time. The reps who attended the Detroit training were very dissatisfied, complained a lot and even abused the trainers.

Somehow management identified that it was me who was making the big difference and wanted to send me to Detroit. I refused. I told them that my classes were happy because I was happy. I was happy because I was able to go to Sedona every weekend and recharge my spiritual batteries. Put me in a cement skyrise in Detroit and I would be just as miserable as the rest.

I completed that assignment and moved to Sedona. About six months later the same client contacted me again and wanted me to come to Detroit for the month of June and attend some meetings. This seemed unusual. I wasn't asked to design any new training programs. They just wanted me to be there and attend the meetings. I pressed for further clarity on what they wanted me to "do" because they seemed to be willing to pay me a lot of money to "just be" there. I was told, "Just do what you do. You know what you do. Just do that." Again I had to meditate to find out what this was all about. My inner guidance told me that at some level they acknowledged that my presence made a significantly positive difference. The meetings ran more smoothly, were more fun, harmonious and more productive when I was around. The clients felt more confident, grounded and peaceful when I was present. Even though they couldn't articulate it, they felt it and were willing to pay me for it.

You can do something like this wherever you are right now. Here is another example. Let's say you are a plumber or handyman. The next time you fix a showerhead, you can set the intention that when the people of the house take a shower, liquid light bathes their aura and washes away anger, fear and judgment. Or if you unclog a drain, you can set the intention that unclogging the drain in the house also unclogs any obstacles in the people, allowing energy to flow freely through their systems. **You can make any activity sacred.**

When you bring your God/Goddess Cell and your Divine Plan into your body and reprogram your mind to align with it, you will begin receiving an unending flow of ideas — all creative expressions of your true nature. *Divine Humans* **act** on these ideas and bring them full into form in the physical world. That is why I said you'll be busy.

A *Divine Human* is in partnership with Spirit — your own Family of Light. It's a 50/50 partnership so you have to do your part and Spirit will do theirs. And guess what? You are the one that's in the physical world, so you get to do the physical half. Spirit can whisper great ideas in your ear, but you have to act on them. Spirit can set up wonderfully magical synchronistic events, but you still have to walk through the open doors and follow where they lead. You can't sit back and expect that Spirit is going to bring you a big wad of money and deposit it in your lap. The Source of All That Is will pay you abundantly for fulfilling your Divine Plan. That's your new job.

Journey's End

You have memories of a past life that was filled with struggle, fear and pain. You notice that as every day goes by, those memories are fading. The emotional attachment is gone. The old story no longer feels real. It feels like no more than a video you watched a long time ago.

There may be certain thoughts come to mind that seem very familiar from the past. But they have no emotional charge and you are not driven by them anymore. They hardly seem to make sense any more. The past no longer binds you, so you can enter each new moment with a sense of wonder and excitement. Experiment, take risks. You know that you are Divine Love and your actions will not be judged. You know that death is an illusion, so there is nothing to lose in venturing out. You know that you are deeply connected to the inner wisdom and all-knowing qualities of your I AM Presence. Your internal guidance system is strong and getting stronger every day.

If in your past fear-based life, you had addictions or compulsive thoughts or behaviors, you see these lose their hold on you, lose their control over you. You see that there is no way that you will slip back into the fear-based reality. You are having too much fun in your joy-based reality, which is getting stronger and stronger everyday.

The journey ends when you embody *Sacred Union*. When you embody *Sacred Union*, you are the *Source* and the *Center of Creation*. All creation comes to you. The illusion of time and space dissolves. There is no where else to go. You stand still, and all creation comes to you. Then you are free to enjoy the rest of your life, an Ascended Master embodied, co-creating your version of Paradise on Earth.

I paved the way. The road is clearly marked. I've given you the sign posts to look for along the way. I'll be here waiting for you at your journey's end. Hurry up. I want more playmates!

Part Two

My Sacred Union Journey

"Are you living your soul's purpose?" It's a powerful question. If you ask it of yourself, be ready to change in a big way. It's the question that led me on a magical, transformational journey from Detroit, Michigan, to the island paradise of Kaua'i.

It seems like only a few years ago (1997), I was in a secure 22-year marriage with two healthy, well-adjusted teenage children. My career was at its peak. I was making a very comfortable salary as a business consultant in the Detroit auto industry, specializing in the design of corporate training programs and leading large-scale change initiatives. My work was respected and my consulting skills considered valuable. I lived in a beautiful home in an affluent neighborhood, with a car for each member of the family, enjoying two-week vacations in the Caribbean each year. By all standards I was self-actualized; I should have felt fulfilled and happy, but that was not the case.

Some call it midlife crisis. My husband, Dave, did! For me, it was much more than that. I wanted to go deeper. Where was the magic, the adventure, the mystery? **Where was the passion**? I felt disconnected from anything that seemed truly important. I longed for true intimacy. And this question kept coming into my consciousness: "Are you living your soul's purpose?" I had to ask myself, "Was I really put on this earth to train guys to sell more cars?"

For the past 25 years, I had been on a spiritual quest, seeking, mostly through books, a deeper understanding of how our reality worked. Sensing an intelligent consciousness behind the seemingly random events, I wondered why some people seemed naturally lucky and blessed while others seemed cursed to one bad break after the other. Still others seemed to exhibit an exquisite balance between grace and sorrow. Even in my youth, I remember listening and watching others closely. I pondered the link between people's beliefs and what really showed up in their lives. I came to the conclusion that whatever you believe — it is true — for you.

Voraciously, I digested books that proposed metaphysical explanations to reality, preferring them over what the hard core scientists proposed — which to me seemed incomplete at best.

By age 42, I felt that I had fully executed a major life contract. There was the sense that one phase of my life was now complete and another phase — vastly different from the first — was waiting to be born.

"Am I really following the calling of my heart?" I asked myself this question. I found myself suffocating in my own sense of safety and security. Where was the mystery? Where was the adventure? Where was the passion for life I experienced as a child? I was drowning in the sameness, not feeling anything. My husband called me Spock (the Vulcan from Star Trek who doesn't have emotions). I was denying my anger, my sadness, my grief and guilt. I was questioning my worthiness to really have the life I wanted.

On his 43rd birthday in July 1993, my husband, Dave, announced his "Two Year Plan." He told me, "In two years, I'm leaving. You can come with me if you want, but even if you don't, I'm leaving." This came as quite a shock as I thought that we had been sharing a happy marriage for the past 18 years. So I asked him, "Who are you leaving? What are you leaving? What do you mean — leaving?" He explained that he was referring to his family business and said, "If I don't leave by the time I'm 45, I never will."

Dave had always expressed dissatisfaction with job in the family business that his parents created 50 years before. It was their dream come true, not his. He felt that he fell into it by default and was stuck. I had always encouraged him to find and follow his own dream. So after getting over the initial shock of the words "I'm leaving," I told him that I was happy to go along with him and support him in pursuing a new life outside of the family business. I asked him why he didn't do it now, instead of waiting two years. He said, "It will take me two years to work up the courage and find something else to do."

One of the things we both looked forward to was our vacation to the Caribbean each year. Dave would spend the whole year pouring over travel books, picking out an island to visit and then developing a detailed itinerary. When we are on our vacation, we would check out the island to see if it was somewhere we wanted to live. At home, we turned our Florida Room into a Caribbean Room, decorating it with treasures we bought there. Dave made pen and ink drawings inspired by photographs of the island streets and buildings. He was quite good at it. I offered my encouragement by framing his art and mounting it on the walls around our Caribbean Room.

Especially dear to my heart was our weekly 'date night.' Every Friday night, Dave would take over the cooking. He would grill fish and make delicious rum punches from a recipe we discovered on our travels. We played Jimmy Buffet and reggae music, ate dinner in the Caribbean room, danced and dreamed out loud about creating a new life in the Caribbean. These date nights were the happiest times of my marriage.

The next two years came and went without any change. From time to time, I checked in with Dave to see if he was any closer to finding his heart's calling and how and when he might leave his family business and create a new life. I offered encouragement. I made suggestions. He saw this input as annoying, rather than supportive.

During those two years I had discovered the concept of "creating your own reality." I immersed myself in *The Abraham Material* channeled by Esther Hicks. I practiced conscious manifestation and had a lot of success influencing the little things in my life.

By the time the New Year rang in 1995, I felt confident in my manifesting abilities and suggested to Dave that we consciously create a blueprint for a new life together. I reasoned that there would surely be more power behind two people manifesting than one. Since the manifestation involved a new life together, we should both be in on it. He agreed and we spent hours on New Year's Day visualizing, energizing and launching a written blueprint for a new life together in the Caribbean.

In March, I manifested my dream job working as an instructional designer in a consulting firm that was known for only hiring "the cream of the crop." In August, my client asked me to develop a proposal and work plan for training their car dealers in the Caribbean and South American markets. They estimated that there were 50 dealers and each one needed a week of training. They wanted a plan that included contracting a trainer for a year, and anticipated renewing the contract each year, for the next three years. This was the ticket, the opportunity, the open door Dave and I had created. I was so excited. I could be the one to deliver the training. We could have a steady, dependable income while living in the Caribbean.

When I told Dave, he got a "glazed over" look in his eyes. It didn't seem like the good news was registering. He didn't seem excited. He wouldn't talk about how we were going to make the transition. I thought that he doubted it would actually happen and he didn't want to get his hopes up. So in an effort to prove it's legitimacy, I brought home written proposals, detailed work plans and budgets all approved and signed by the VP. But every time I brought up the subject, the glazed eyes returned.

When it got to the point in the process where I needed to tell my manager and the client that I wanted the training assignment for myself, I confronted Dave. It was then he admitted that he was too afraid to walk into the new life we had created. He said no to our dream.

I was devastated. My devastation turned to anger when I had to hire another trainer to follow my dream. These words kept echoing in the halls of my heart, "If I don't leave by the time I'm 45, I never will. Never will. Never will….."

It took me a while to recuperate. Now that I knew for sure that I could manifest big life-changing dreams, there was no way I could stay stuck in a life that was anything less than everything I wanted. Sadly, I began to loose respect for Dave. I judged him as being a coward and a betrayer of our dream. I began to notice that almost all of his life force energy was spent trying to avoid fear and guilt.

It was also during this time that I learned that other people in my life act as a mirror for what is going on inside me. With this new understanding, I realized that no matter what choices Dave made, I still had the opportunity, the power and the obligation to myself, to create my own life, just the way I wanted it. I couldn't continue to use Dave as a scapegoat for my own fear of change.

Then things shifted. It began when I asked Spirit, "What have I come here to do?" The answer surprised me: "Your purpose and path are in the direction of your joy. Follow your joy and you will realize your purpose." I then surrendered to my own Divine Plan and vowed to let go of everything that didn't support my purpose. I mean **everything**. The first challenge was to find out what brought me joy.

I met a woman, Verlaine Crawford, at a conference where she inspired me with her stories of manifesting and making peace with your subpersonalities (those split-off, disassociated pieces of yourself). In her book, *Ending the Battle Within*, Verlaine suggests writing the script for the life you really desire. During our 10-day Caribbean vacation in the spring of 1996, I decided to write a new blueprint for my life. This is the script I wrote for myself.

Self-Expression

> The universe pays me abundantly for expressing my passion for life each day. I sing, I dance, I write, I heal, I teach, I compose heavenly music, I channel unconditional love and wisdom. I feel the creative vitality of life coursing through me.

Travel

> I travel to beautiful, exotic places at times when the weather is sunny and warm. I spend just enough time in each place to experience the beauty, meet and enjoy wonderful people and learn about the unique aspects of the culture. I am welcomed as an ambassador of love and tranquility wherever I go. Traveling from place to place is always easy, comfortable and safe.

Home

> I live in a beautiful home that is simple, lovely and comfortable. The climate is warm and sunny most of the time and I feel completely safe here. Food and other supplies that add to my comfort and enjoyment are easy to

acquire and are in abundant supply. The view from my home is breathtakingly beautiful, with water and mountains, sunrises and sunsets. This place on Earth enhances my feeling of tranquility, creativity and strength. My home echoes my favorite colors, designs and tastes and is filled with wonderful artwork that I have collected from my travels around the world.

Abundance

I am an abundant being. All of the good things in life are attracted to me in abundant supply. I enjoy an abundance of comfort, security, love, joy, peace, wisdom, freedom, friendship, beauty, play and money.

Relationships

All of my relationships are based on unconditional love, truth and integrity. I enjoy a deepening intimacy with all life, including people, nature and spirit. My relationships nurture and support my true essence. Because I feel nourished, I freely and joyfully support others. Every day I am finding more and more joy in my relationships.

I wrote that in 1996 while on vacation in the Caribbean with my husband. It took me all day as I dialoged with all the subpersonalities that expressed themselves, casting fear and doubt that I could create such a wonderful life. Yet using Verlaine's technique, I was able to negotiate with all the voices and come to consensus. Together, my subpersonalities and I launched our manifestation with great ceremony.

Dave seemed uninterested in the new life for which I had written the new script. He didn't even ask to see it, so I assumed that he didn't want to be part of it. Saddened, I decided to move on regardless.

After launching my manifestation, I announced my one-year plan to Dave. "In one year, I'm leaving. You are welcome to come with me if you want. And I hope you do. But even if you don't…. in one year I'm leaving."

Every day during that next year I found ways to remind Dave that I was going to create a new life. For the first six months, I always included him in the plans I talked about. He would nod in agreement with the same glazed-over eyes I had seen before. So in the second six months, whenever he talked about the future, usually including me, I gently reminded him that I would not be there. His response was always the same — "Oh yeah." — followed by the glazed eyes.

My one-year plan was approaching its fourth quarter. On February 21, 1997 I was scheduled to receive an intuitive reading with my first spiritual teacher. I had taken many intuitive development and past life-regression classes with her. It was my tradition to receive one intuitive reading from her per year. On this night I asked about my relationship with Dave. She told me that our soul's contract with each other was complete. She said that she saw no energetic or emotional connections between us at all. She said, "When I put you on the timeline and watch you walk forward, you will just not stay together. If I try to force you to stay together, I see that you unconsciously create a terminal illness and leave your body and the relationship that way."

Wow. Our contract is complete! Leave the relationship or die! It was going to take a while to integrate that information.

The next morning I woke up and felt my body going into contractions. Waves of energy moved up my spine and the feeling was like the labor of childbirth. It lasted for about an hour and a half. Because a strong spiritual guidance has always been an active force in my life, I uttered a silent prayer, a call for help, asking, "What is happening to me?" The answer was clear. "You are giving birth to yourself."

At that time, I was seeing a massage therapist every other week. As luck would have it, I had an appointment the day after my birthing experience. I didn't mention it and only asked her to check in and see if she noticed anything different. When she was finished, she told me that she was very sensitive to people's energy and knew that if she was blindfolded, she could differentiate between each one of her clients. She said, "There is nothing about your energy that is familiar." I asked her if she had ever seen this before. She said, "Yes, twice. Both times it was with women who had just become pregnant. It's like a new soul has come into your body."

My mind was changing rapidly; but emotionally I felt unable to break the ties and commitments that had bound me for 22 years. I struggled with all the conventional questions: I was married to a good man; how could I leave him? How could I leave my children and all my so-called responsibilities? What would my parents say? What would my employer say? How would I be judged? How could I live with the guilt of thrusting all my loved ones into a vortex of change?

There was a new sense of priority in my life — an extreme desire to focus on spiritual service. I didn't know exactly how that should look, but I seemed driven to find my soul's purpose and to learn how to live it.

To me, the internal changes were monumental. But I didn't realize how much I changed in the eyes of others, until one day, only four months later. My daughter said, "Who are you? Your personality has changed so much. There is nothing about you that I recognize. You are somebody else in my mother's body."

She certainly hit the nail on the head. It was my first clue that I had what is now commonly referred to as a "walk-in" experience. A higher aspect of me was born into my body which I later learned was the feminine aspect of my Oversoul Matrix. In some rare cases, there is actually a totally new soul that comes into to replace the first. But most often it is a higher aspect of the original soul. It seems like a totally new soul because you begin a whole new lifetime while still in the same body. There is no need to die and be reborn. It was at that point, I took the first bold step and claimed the right to spend a month in Sedona.

Sedona Calls

Sedona, Arizona called me, and I responded. It was the first of many times a place would draw me to it. In this instance, I was invited to attend a week-long workshop and then spend another three weeks touring the Southwest in a motor coach. When I received the invitation, every cell in my body jumped for joy and said, "YES." Then it seemed like everyone I talked to brought up the subject of Sedona. Every time I picked up a magazine or looked at a newspaper, there was something written on Sedona or pictures of Sedona. Every time it came to my awareness, my emotions would soar.

Even though my being loved the idea, there was much resistance from my family. My husband, Dave, couldn't agree I should leave for a whole month — a week maybe, but not a month. My 16-year old daughter's tears tugged at my heart as she echoed the words of her father. My parents felt I was misguided and something was wrong if I felt the need to go off for a month to "find myself."

Only my son, then 17, seemed supportive. He was going off to college soon and understood the need to leave familiar surroundings in order to come to a sense of self. Kathy, my manager and mentor at the consulting firm I worked for, was also very encouraging, advising me to take the leave of absence that she sensed I needed. Riddled with fear and guilt, I evoked the courage to do it anyway. Nobody could deter me.

Sedona was everything I expected and more. Magic was everywhere. The mysterious sculptor who created the red-rock monuments must sit back and watch in silent amusement as the residents and tourist glide, and sometimes fumble, their way through the myriad of synchronistic events. The veils seem much thinner there as you watch your thoughts become manifest almost instantly. I made friends easily. Everybody spoke my language — the language of spirit, healing and conscious manifestation. A language I now refer to as "Temple Talk." Indeed, many priests and priestess of ancient wisdom pass through Sedona on their journey back to Self.

I spent that month meditating, grieving, and sampling the myriad of healing techniques by many soul practitioners. This allowed me to sort through my thoughts and feelings and separate what my soul really wanted from the social programming I had adopted. It took even more courage to go back to Michigan, and bring my life there to completion. For I had decided to start over again, with my new Self, in Sedona.

Hoping to make a relatively graceful exit, I stayed in Detroit for the next seven months while I integrated the thoughts and feelings of my new soul stream.

One night I came home from work and was the only one in the house. All of a sudden, I felt a strong presence in the room. I looked around and nobody was there. Yet the feeling of a presence was so strong. This had never happened before, but I knew that spiritual beings can make their presence known. So I called out and asked, "Who's there?" In my mind, I heard the very clear reply, "We have come to support you. You will be getting some bad news later tonight. And we want you to know we are here for you." It was my impression that it was Archangel Michael and some others that I couldn't identify.

You would think that kind of message would freak me out and send me into imagining what the bad news could be. I believe the angels transmitted some peaceful energy to me, because I acknowledged the message, expressing my gratitude for their support and then promptly forgot all about it.

The family came home and we had our usual dinner together — nothing out of the ordinary. Then Dave asked me to go for a walk. He said he had something he wanted to talk to me about.

During our walk, Dave asked me to explain how and why I had changed so much. He told me that my personality was different and that I seemed like a different person. For the first time, I shared my February 22 rebirth experience. It told him I didn't really understand it well myself, but it seemed to me that a new soul had come to live in my body. I told him the new soul's name was Suzanna. He told me he didn't like Suzanna and wanted his old Suzanne back.

It wasn't until that moment that I really knew, deep down, that any hope I had for my marriage was gone. In that moment, I felt Archangel Michael's energy enter my body. His strength and compassion filled my heart with such intensity, I thought it would burst. Calmly, I told Dave, "Your old Suzanne is gone. I don't know where she is and I can't get her back, even if I wanted to. And I don't want to, because I like my new self a whole lot better."

At this point, Dave got very emotional and said a lot of nasty things. But with Michael's support, I did not experience it as hurtful. I clearly saw that Dave was reacting out of grief and fear. I knew that I would have the support and strength I needed to see this transition through. I prayed that Dave would too. He interpreted the peaceful, quiet response, born of my compassion, as coldness and a lack of feeling. Nothing could be further from the truth, yet I knew he wanted to cling to his perception.

In his mind he began creating a new version of reality. In his story, he cast me as the cold, calculating bitch. He cast himself as the poor, unsuspecting, heartbroken victim who is suddenly cast aside without any warning or good reason. He came to like that story, and in the months and years to come, he told it often, until he believed it was true. He forgot that he was the first one to talk about leaving. He forgot that I had invited him, almost everyday for four years, to create a new life with me.

Yet, I will never forget, that at some level, it was Dave who first recognized that our soul contract was complete. As a parting gift, he set in motion those forces that would move me down the path of my destiny. If he had not registered his feelings of being trapped in someone else's idea of what his life should be, I would not have recognized my own. So it is with great gratitude that I recognize him as a wonderful catalyst for my spiritual evolution. He played out his role perfectly without even knowing it. He served as an alarm clock for me, while staying asleep himself. Brilliant!

In those months leading up to my departure from Detroit, I kept getting visual snapshots and emotional flashes of what my new life would be like. It was so different from my current life, I would go into extreme "overwhelm" trying to figure out how to get from here to there. The uncertainty and anxiety would paralyze me for days. Feeling depressed at my lack of movement, I would feel more urgency and the anxiety would grow, creating a vicious circle.

Prayer always works for me, so I prayed to take away the sense of urgency. I prayed to ease up on the 'big picture.' I asked for just enough guidance and just enough energy to make it through one day at a time. Each morning I would ask for inspiration on what to do that day, and then I followed that guidance and found there was always enough energy to support the specified tasks.

Emotionally, I still needed help with separating from the past and all the ties that no longer served the new life I was creating. Again I prayed for help. I was led to a process called *Integrative Natural Healing*, facilitated by Adam El David. His individual sessions helped me to let go of the limiting thoughts, beliefs, feelings, and attitudes that I had accumulated regarding myself, and particularly, myself in relationships. I was able to release the anger and blame I carried regarding male relationships in my life, including my father, my son, my husband, teachers and even my vision of a male God and the male aspect of myself. In the same way, I performed an emotional clearing around all the female relationships in my life.

I spent a lot of time asking myself all those judgmental questions I knew others would ask me. "How can you leave your children?" "How can you give up a marriage of 22 years?" "How will you make money?" I struggled with each question until I was able to let go of the underlying beliefs that were causing the limitations and guilt. I came to the realization, through this process of growth and integration, that if I am not true to myself, I'm no good to anyone.

There was one occasion that seemed to mark a breakthrough. It was the day I told my parents that I was getting a divorce and moving to Sedona. My parents asked me, in very fearful and judgmental tones, all the questions that I had been asking myself. But I was prepared and able to answer each question with confidence, standing firm within myself. I was not triggered by their fear. Instead I felt courage. I was not triggered by their judgment. Instead I felt excitement about the new life I was creating.

In exasperation, my father spat out the venomous pronouncement, "You are in love with yourself!" I said, "Yes, as a matter of fact I AM. Thank you for noticing." He walked out of the room in confusion and frustration. Later that day, my father came back. He hugged me and said, "I don't understand what you are doing, but I love you." Unconditional love — there's nothing else like it. Start with yourself and then you will see it reflected back to you through others.

While it certainly is not the only path to integration and self-awareness, the *Integrative Natural Healing Program* was the opportunity I found to clear some core beliefs that no longer served me. Through it, I was able to experience a sense of "fullness" and completeness within myself, activating a passion for all of life. And I was left with a truly beautiful gift: self-love.

Raised to believe I must be "self-less" I believed that it was wrong to put myself first. Sound familiar? But how can we possibly nourish another if we come from a place of emptiness? When I come from a place of fullness, what I share with others is what overflows from within me. In fact, when I am in my fullness, I have a burning desire to share with others, rather than a sense of stinginess. It becomes an urge, almost a requirement, of living.

The process gave me the courage to make the changes I knew I had to make in my life to align with my soul's purpose. It gave me strength, and it gave me trust.

A new sense of personal integrity set in when I realized how important it was to live life authentically. Yet, we are socialized to believe it is more important to "fit in" and not "rock the boat." At every turn, we are encouraged to give our personal power away and conform.

It took me only a few months to move through a relatively graceful divorce, to earn a comfortable property settlement for my 22 years of living the American dream in metropolitan suburbia.

I continued my corporate job, landing a temporary assignment that took me to Scottsdale, Arizona for five months. From there, I visited Sedona every weekend. From Friday afternoon to Monday morning I rented a room in the home of Paol Seagram, a successful Sedona artist and spiritual teacher. I communed with the red rocks and established a friendly support network with people who would become my new spiritual family.

When the assignment ended, I resigned as a staff consultant, and was able to continue serving my clients as a subcontractor. The move from Michigan to Sedona was one of the scariest and yet most exhilarating changes I ever made. I loved Sedona, with its red rocks and clear blue skies. Its transformational electromagnetic energy was juicy and palpable. It was the first time in my life that I felt really connected to Blessed Mother Earth. Intuitively, I knew the move to Sedona was temporary, but necessary for my healing and transformation. At the time, I thought I would stay in Sedona for two months, complete my transformation, and then move to a Caribbean island.

Answering Sedona's Call

For the first two months, I did some house sitting in Oak Creek Canyon. At the end of two months, there was no way I was ready to leave. When I checked with my inner guidance, I was told to go ahead and settle in, "you'll be here for a while." By this time, Paol Seagram, who I had been staying with on the weekends, had become a dear friend. He offered to rent me a room in his home on a more long-term basis. It felt so easy to move in with my spiritual brother and the loving support that he offered.

As I moved four boxes and my computer into my room (the only worldly possessions that I brought from Michigan), I felt my energy field being embraced by the house. I felt a melding as my energy expanded to every corner of the house and we merged. Another friend, Jennifer, noticed this energy melding between the house and me. She had just commented on it when Paol came out of his bedroom and announced, "I'm done with Sedona. Do you want to take over the lease on this house?"

It was not unusual for Paol to make sudden major life-change decisions at the beckoning of his own inner guidance. Still, I was shocked and more than a little afraid to lose, immediately, the security blanket that I believed he would provide. Quickly I learned that the energy of Sedona strips you of all of your illusions of security and continually offers up practice exercises of trust, trust and ever-deepening levels of trust.

I trusted that somehow, I would be able to make a rental payment that was twice what my mortgage payment had been. Synchronicity running high, I soon met a woman who would become my roommate, friend and eased the transition.

Paol asked if he could leave his furniture and other "stuff" there because he didn't know yet where he would settle. Of course, this was wonderful for me, because without it I would have only an empty house to live in. He warned me that someday he would call and say, "I'm coming for my stuff." I put out a prayer that when that call came, it would be easy and affordable for me to replace the contents of the house.

The call came four months later. I renewed my prayer and then let it go. Later, the very same day, I was guided to call a woman regarding a retreat center she had advertised. As it turned out, the retreat center had been shut down due to zoning changes and she was having a large estate sale. I completely outfitted my empty house in one day. To add to my good fortune, the woman told me that everything in the house was only one year old. Without the retreat business, she had no means of income, and had to let it all go quickly. I got a house full of almost new "stuff" for 25 cents on the dollar.

Sedona was very good to me and I flourished there. My circle of friends expanded. I felt nourished by the very potent creative energy radiated by the musicians, artists and healers I hung out with. From time to time I would get called back to Detroit for a training job. These jobs always arrived within days of praying for the means to manifest a particular desire. At one point, I had decided to take my children to Europe for a vacation and estimated it would cost $10,000. The next day, I got a call from a client with a job that would pay $10,000.

The veils seemed thinner in Sedona. It seemed easier to hear my inner guidance. It certainly was easier to follow it, because none of my new friends knew the "old me" so they didn't try to keep me contained in a well-known identity. As a matter of fact, because like attracts like, all of my new friends were going through transformation, practicing balance in the face of change and TRUST. We took turns holding compassionate space for each other as we shed the layers of the onion we called our identity.

Drawn back into the *Integrative Natural Healing* work (the sessions that helped me launch my new life); I became a facilitator of this process. I learned that there are five core issues that all of us in human bodies need to release and heal.

Five Core Issues

By Adam El-David. Reprinted by permission.

1. Feminine Issues

Inherent in all of us are severe, yet reasonable negative attitudes regarding why women (and feminine energy) cannot be trusted. This would include the feminine aspect of God (Goddess), your genetic mothers, sisters, wives, daughters, lovers, your own feminine aspects of intuition, receptivity, sensuality, nurturing, all the women you have ever loved, know or been throughout all time, all dimensions. These attitudes include feelings of hatred, anger, jealousy, envy, abandonment and betrayal. During the clearing process, these negative states are transformed into open-hearted trust and acceptance toward all things feminine in nature, essence and form.

2. Masculine Issues

Likewise, we all carry negative attitudes regarding why males (and male energy) cannot be trusted. This would include the male aspect of God, your fathers, brothers, sons, husbands, lovers, your own male aspects of protector, provider, giver, initiator of action, and any male you have ever know, loved or been throughout all time, all dimensions. It would also include the patriarchal aspects of our society such as government, religion, education, financial institutions, etc. These attitudes include feelings of hatred, anger, jealousy, envy, abandonment and betrayal. During the clearing process, these negative states are transformed into open-hearted trust and acceptance toward all things masculine in nature, essence and form.

3. Fear

The fear patterns include all manner of instituted fear used to control behavior from a religious, political or social point of view. This would include fear of life and death, fear of success and failure, fear of light and darkness, fear of intimate relations with yourself and others. During the clearing process, this pattern is transformed into open-hearted, blatant courage.

4. Guilt

There are the destroyers of self-worth, which keep all of us from rising to the Divine Self Image that is our right to inherit from the Creator. Guilt, self-judgment, self-denial and self-pity prevent us from enjoying life to the fullest. This pattern is transformed into open-hearted, radiant joy.

5. Pain

The deepest level of suppression deals with all the ancient wounds that we bring back over and over again into each lifetime. The activities of hurt, pain, sorrow and grief constantly create upheaval and conflict in our work and personal relationships. These disruptive patterns are transformed into open-hearted, unconditional love and deep compassion toward self.

Adam created a clearing session for each of the Five Core Issues. He combined his extensive background in Rebirthing with Brian Grattan's Mahatma teaching. I had experienced rebirthing, which in itself is a very powerful healing technique. By using a particular kind of breath for a sustained period of time, you unlock cellular memory and release hidden and suppressed thought patterns, emotions, past-life experiences, etc.

Think of it this way. Whenever you are surprised or experience an intense situation, you hold your breath. The thoughts and feelings you are having at that moment are locked into your emotional and mental bodies and stay there until they are expressed. We are socialized to hold on to our intense thoughts and feelings. "Don't rock the boat." "Be nice." "If you can't say anything nice, don't say anything."

Over time, our emotional and mental bodies start to fill up with these suppressed thoughts and feelings. When they stay in our emotional and mental bodies for a long time, they eventually move into the physical body where they create a blockage to the flow of energy in your body. Where ever energy doesn't flow freely through your body, a potential for physical imbalance, disharmony or disease exists.

It makes sense that if you held your breath to lock in thoughts and emotions; conscious breathing could unlock them as well. When you use a Rebirthing breath, the energy goes to places in the physical, emotional, mental and spiritual body (four-body system) where the blockages are and blasts through them. With the blockages clear, energy flows freely and the four-body system has a chance to come back into balance and harmony.

Rebirthing sessions can be very intense because as the energy moves into a blockage to release it, you may re-experience whatever situation occurred when you created the blockage. Many people re-experience their own birth because of the trauma caused by bright lights, burning solutions in your eyes, slaps on the behind and being separated from your mother.

In my first rebirthing session I re-experienced the birth of my daughter. I was able to release the anger and frustration I felt with the hospital staff and my husband during her birth. In another session, I re-experienced what must have been a past-life memory related to being hunted and persecuted as a witch when I was actually a mid-wife and herbalist. With Rebirthing, you never know what will "come up" or when you will finally be clear.

Adam also studied with Brian Grattan, who wrote *Mahatma II*. Mahatma is the name for an aspect of The Source of All That Is. Imagine the breath of Source. In one exhale, Source creates all that is and it moves out into creation to experience life. In the next inhale, all of creation begins moving back into union, merging back into undifferentiated Source. Mahatma is the name of the inhale aspect of Source.

Brian taught that you could call Mahatma consciousness into your body. When you merge with this consciousness, you can then use command statements to direct energy and change the DNA and four-body system. By combining the command statements and the breathwork, Adam created a way to systematically move through the human condition and consciously direct your own clearing. This was a very empowering and potent combination. I loved the way Adam wove these two technologies together. I was initiated into the Mahatma energy and sanctioned by Adam to facilitate the *Five Core Issue* Clearing Sessions.

He sent me the scripts for the sessions and empowered me to begin my own apprenticeship with Spirit. I began the clearing sessions practicing on my friends, those brave souls, who must have been specifically selected by Spirit to give me a baptism by fire.

Adam told me to do the clearings in a specific sequence, but he didn't tell me why. When my friend, Amy, begged me to clear fear issues first, because that was really "up" for her, I allowed myself to be swayed. We did the clearing on fear first and it went very well. She was high on the energies for a couple of weeks afterward.

Then one morning she called me in tears. Her boyfriend had just announced that he was moving to the South Pacific on business, for an undetermined amount of time. This triggered all her mistrust of men and the world in general. When she called me she was saying, "I hate God, I hate men, I hate myself, I don't want to be here anymore, and I just want to die."

When I got to her home, I found her near death. Her body temperature was alarmingly low, she was pale as a ghost and she was hardly breathing. I had to remind her to breathe. I never knew that you could just will yourself to die. On the other hand, I knew deep down she didn't really want to leave, otherwise why would she have called me?

I decided to do the first clearing on male issues because she said she hated God and it was a male that had triggered this reaction. She released A LOT of yucky stuff and by the end of the session the hatred and anger where gone. Do you know that passage in the bible about 'walking through the valley of the shadow of death?' Well, I walked through it with her, and it's not a pretty sight. We came through it into a big void. Not caring now, at all, for anything, Amy was still barely in her body. I prayed for guidance. I couldn't believe what I was told, "If she wants to leave, let her. Bring her to the light and let her decide if that's what she really wants."

142

Talk about trusting! I had to trust that Spirit knew what it was doing. I had to trust myself to believe what I was hearing. I had to trust Amy that she wouldn't leave before her time. Oh my God! What would I do if she decided to leave? I didn't even know how to contact her family. She had a seven-year-old son. What would I do with him? She's one of my best friends and I don't want to lose her. These were the thoughts that were running through my head. Yet, I followed the guidance I heard inside and took her to the light. It was a major breakthrough for me, as well as Amy.

She decided not to leave. When I took her to the light she said, "It's blue and cold. God doesn't live here. There is no love here." I told her to ask the light if this is where she would go if she left her body now. The light said "Yes" and she said "No thanks." I asked her to ask the blue light what she needed. She talked to the light and then asked if I had a session on self-pity. So we did the session on clearing self-judgment, guilt and self-pity. At the end of that session, she came back into her body. I gave her water — she was terribly dehydrated — and made her something to eat. She had a complete turnaround. Before I left, she was laughing as she did a Tarot card reading for me!

She called me every morning after that and told me about all the wonderful insights and clearings she kept having. She said she felt like a newborn baby — full of wonder and excited anticipation. She knew all the fear and anger and hatred were gone.

I did another session with her to clear the mistrust of feminine energy and three others to clear pain, sorrow and grief. She was the first person I took through the all five clearing sessions. It was fun to watch her transformation.

She let go of the old boyfriend, who by the way, was abusive. They didn't resonate with each other after she cleared her fear issues. There is a universal law called the Law of Attraction — like attracts like. We always hear that opposites attract, but that is only a physical law and applies to magnetic attractions. Emotionally, mentally and spiritually — like attracts like. Amy and her boyfriend were originally unconsciously attracted to each other around the issue of suppressed fear. When she released her fear, there was no attractive energy holding the relationship together.

Unfortunately, we've been socialized to create some "good reason" why we have to break up. Our egos create a little psychodrama to give us a good reason. In Amy's case, she could have allowed this separation to be graceful. She could have said goodbye, waving her handkerchief in the air as he sailed away to the South Seas. But she was unaccustomed to graceful endings and co-created a little drama where she triggered his anger and he gave her a black eye. Now she had a good reason to separate.

We don't have to create these dramatic separations. Separations are going to happen. They happen because we don't resonate with each other anymore — plain and simple. We can just let the relationship go with love and gratitude for the soul growth it brought to us.

It's been several years now since I began facilitating these clearings. I've seen it happen over and over again. Whoever or whatever is in your life now is attracted to you at your current frequency and consciousness. When you raise your frequency and expand your consciousness, you change your attraction energy. In order to make room in your life for those people and situations that resonate with you at a higher frequency, you have to be willing to gracefully release the ones that no longer serve you.

During the two years I lived in Sedona my circle of friends and acquaintances changed several times. Every once in a while I wished for a lover or playmate, knowing that I was not ready for any steady romantic relationship. One numerologist told me not to expect to be in partnership for the next two years. He said, "A guy would have to have a jetpack on his back to keep up with you. You are going through a highly accelerated growth period and after it levels off, you can create a partnership if you want."

Every few months I did manifest a playmate. These relationships never lasted long, but were very sweet and playful. I always looked at who I had attracted to see what kind of progress I was making. Pleased with my progress, I was content with this arrangement for the time being. My playmates and I allowed the separations to be graceful and I was always grateful for the gifts shared while we were together.

My apprenticeship with Spirit continued. Whenever I facilitated a clearing session, my client and I would both go into an altered state of consciousness. When in this state, it was even easier for me to hear guidance from my unseen teachers. They showed me images and visions and taught me new things to try with each client.

I continued to work on myself using the *Mahatma II* book by Brian Grattan and other books on ascension written by Joshua David Stone. Both used similar methods of calling for higher initiations, frequencies, light levels and expanded states of consciousness. Initially I didn't experience anything they described in the books — like visits from Ascended Masters who brought gifts and information. But I kept asking for the energy anyway.

Well, my request for initiations must have been on back order because one day, while sitting in meditation with a friend, I received about 20 initiations, one right after another. The meditation lasted more than six hours. I recognized them as the same initiations I had called for. First I would feel a wave of a new, unfamiliar energy wash through me. Then I would hear an explanation of what was happening and see visual images. It was an intense experience, but one that I relished. My friend kept asking, "Haven't you had enough yet?" I would say, "No. I've been waiting for this for too long; bring it on."

Each initiation left me forever altered. I learned that an initiation is a transformation from one state of being to another. Just like a caterpillar transforms into a butterfly; it can never go back to being a caterpillar. And why would it want to? But now, it's all new, being a butterfly. It has to learn how to fly and eat differently. It has to make new butterfly friends and friends with the flowers and bees. It has to practice awhile before it masters butterfly consciousness. I learned a lot about the process of initiations, practice and mastery.

The initiations and what I learned from my spiritual teachers while in sessions brought the clearing sessions to the next level of evolvement. I attended a *Melchizedek Method* Facilitator Training with Alton Kamadon and learned how to set a safe and sacred space using sacred geometry and compassion energy. I added guided imagery and initiations to the clearing sessions. These guided dream-like journeys helped my clients release limiting beliefs and stored emotional energy, and to receive information, spiritual gifts, and energy transmissions that would raise their frequencies and expand their consciousness. I synthesized and organized everything I learned and passed it along to my clients through these sessions. Soon I was able to attract enough people to begin conducting the sessions in groups. I developed a curriculum and six to twelve people would move through it together, enjoying the group energy and support.

One of my clients phoned me to let me know that he had just received a session with an *Aura Star 2000*. This is a biofeedback machine with forty sensors that line up with the terminal energy meridians on the tips of the fingers. The machine measures the resistance of energy as it moves through the body. The output is a frequency reading that is translated into color. The software program runs on a laptop or PC and displays the colors on the monitor overlaid on the body, giving you an aura-like reading. Even more impressive is that you can watch these colors change in real-time response to whatever is going on around you.

My client had two readings; one before his clearing session with me, and one after. The difference in the two readings was so impressive, the operator of the machine wanted to meet me and find out what I was doing. Coincidentally, my internal guidance had been encouraging me to check out this technology. But I had kept putting it off. Now, with this nudge, I was ready to investigate.

I went in for my reading. My aura was mostly clear blue-green, the colors of a healer, I am told. My chakras were unusual colors, with pink in my heart center, violet in my throat and two chakras showing up outside my body, above and below me. The operator was able to record the reading on video, so after her standard reading, she let me play a little. I wanted to see how my energy changed in response to the I AM Invocation, which calls your I AM Presence (higher self) into your body.

I recited the invocation: I AM All That Is. I AM All That Is. I AM All That Is. I AM the Source of my creations. I AM the Creator of my reality. I AM Divine Light. I AM Divine Love. I

AM Divine Joy. I AM Divine Peace. I AM Divine Abundance. I AM the being of synthesis and fusion. I AM That I AM.

As I said the invocation, the color around my inner core went from blue-green to emerald green. My chakras expanded. The whole aura pulsated in and out as it adjusted to the new frequencies I was receiving. Then on the last words: I AM That I AM, the whole field suddenly expanded to three times its original size and turned completely gold.

No wonder it feels so good to say that invocation! The I AM Presence is a golden energy. Using this invocation, you can get it to stay in your body for a while, but for most people it doesn't stay very long. The I AM Invocation is used in all of my sessions.

Needless to say, I was quite taken with the *Aura Star 2000*. I wanted one for my own to play with, but when I asked my inner advisors if I should purchase one, the answer was no. It was hard to put out of my mind as I imagined what a great training and marketing tool it could be. Yet I trusted my guidance and put the whole idea on the back burner.

Egypt Calls

One of the dear friends I made in Sedona was Diana James. I recognized our past-life connection as sisters and Priestesses in the Temples of Isis. She is a gifted teacher and a channel for volumes of information on healing with essential oils and communicating with nature spirits to heal disharmony in the environment. I will be forever grateful to her for nudging me in the right direction at certain points on my path. She taught me that sometimes Spirit calls us to certain places for growth, release and expansion. She encouraged me to hear and answer the calls as they presented themselves. I had already answered Sedona's call, but that was only the beginning.

In November 1999, it was Diana that made me aware that Egypt was calling me. Diana was arranging a tour group for her annual spring trip to Egypt and invited me along. My resistance was strong. I did not want to go — not at all. Even though Egypt had fascinated me as an adolescent, I felt that I was "over it." "Not interested." "Can't afford it." "Don't have time." I came up with a dozen excuses why I should not go. Yet when I went inside to ask for guidance, I was told, "Go to Egypt." I made plans to join her in March 2000.

Kaua'i Calls

In December 1999, after a year and a half in the Sedona desert, the tropical air of Hawaii began to call to me. Patti, a friend from Michigan, phoned suggesting we visit Hawaii together. Then I met a new playmate and he shared stories of his many adventures on Kaua'i. At a holiday party, other guests brought up their recent journey to Kaua'i. OK. OK. I get the picture. Kaua'i is calling. I surrendered. Patti and I decided to spend the month of February exploring the Garden Isle of Kaua'i. My schedule for the next year was beginning to take shape.

Answering Kaua'i's Call

On the plane over, I thought I would miss Sedona, but soon found that Kaua'i was made up of the same red dirt and blue skies. Add to that the lush tropical plants, moist salt air, and the ocean. There were strange stirrings within me. Could this be home?

I received my answer on a hike from the Kilauea Lighthouse up to Crater Hill, well known as a sacred Hawaiian power spot and, some say, an inter-dimensional portal. Whatever it is, Crater Hill certainly evoked a strong experience for Patti and me. I began to feel strange waves of energy wash over and through me. Patti had a vision of a past-life where we were both priestesses who sacrificed ourselves to the volcano to save the village. As she spoke about her vision, I had a strong full-bodied truth reaction. Then I heard, very clearly, "Because of your great love, this island will help you manifest anything you want, in grand style."

Immediately we began to see evidence of Mother Kaua'i fulfilling her promise and she seemed to welcome us with open arms. We were staying at a B&B and the owner asked if I could help a friend of hers who suffered from chronic fatigue and hadn't been able to go to work for a few weeks. I said I didn't know how the mental/emotional clearing work I did affected the physical body, but I was willing to give it a shot and see what happened. After her session, this client felt completely restored, went back to work and started telling everybody about the "healer from Sedona" that helped her. People began calling the B&B looking for me. The owner decided to have a reception and invited all her friends. This led to private and group sessions, a radio interview and an offer of sponsorship for a future visit to Kaua'i.

Patti, who has a wonderful singing voice, was "discovered" at a local Karaoke Bar and later was asked to join an all-women band. She was also offered an opportunity to sell timeshares and a place to live. It seemed that the island was setting things up for an easy move. We spent a wonderful month soaking up the energy. It was delicious. Synchronicity ran high and we were heavily seduced by Mother Kaua'i into come back again soon, preferably for good.

To add to the adventure, I often felt a very strange, new energy entering through the top of my head. It felt blissful, but also left me feeling very ungrounded. I was glad to be traveling with Patti, as it would have been difficult for me to navigate on my own in that state. Patti was a wonderful compliment to me. With her very down-to-Earth, Taurus energy, she helped me feel safe and grounded. It felt like my spirit was just moments away from being sucked up out of my body. During these times, Patti would take me to the beach where I would almost bury myself in the sand to avoid floating away.

When I asked my inner guidance what was happening, I was told that I was receiving energy from the dolphins and whales. Later I learned that the cetaceans were calling certain people to ground and anchor the Platinum Ray into the land. I also learned the Platinum Ray came from the Divine Feminine aspect of Source. The dolphins and whales had been grounding the Platinum Ray in the water since the beginning of life on this planet. Now it was time to pass the torch to humans to take over guardianship of the planet.

Near the end of my month on Kaua'i, I started turning my attention to my upcoming visit to Egypt. I would only be home in Sedona for a week before heading off to Egypt for three weeks.

Back To Sedona

When I returned to Sedona, I felt like a totally different person. It felt like, once again, I had died to whatever self image I had and was reborn into something new.

My guidance insisted that I check in with the *Aura Star 2000*. To my amazement, my aura showed up as completely white (or maybe platinum) except for a violet tornado, with the point at my throat and the wide mouth far above my head. It looked like a violet satellite dish. My upper chakras were all white and the lower ones were colored, but not the normal chakra colors in the normal sequence. This was definite proof that something major had happened to me on Kaua'i. I was something new, something different. I vowed to return to the *Aura Star* after my upcoming trip to Egypt.

Answering Egypt's Call

One of the internal messages that often came into my awareness at that time was "Be the Goddess." There seemed to be a lot of Goddess Consciousness both in Sedona and on Kaua'i. At least there were a lot of women running around calling themselves Goddesses. There were men who said they honored the Goddess. A numerologist told me that my purpose was to anchor the feminine aspect of God into the planet and express it as The Goddess.

Great! I still didn't understand what that meant — be the Goddess. Do you have a job description I could look at please? The answer came quite clearly from within — "Go to the temples of Egypt and remember what it feels like to be the Goddess."

I got my first clue on the plane ride from LAX to Cairo. Egyptian Air showed the movie "The Muse." Sharon Stone played a character that inspired men with creativity in exchange for shelter and gifts (preferably from Tiffany's). In her role as muse, she really didn't have to "do" anything. She would just spend time with the men, having them tag along as she flowed from one spontaneous adventure to the next. While in her presence, they would begin to see things from a different perspective and it would ignite their creativity and they would produce masterpieces. This movie gave me the first clue that it was the energetic presence, the freedom, and the sacred attitude of a female that differentiated a Goddess from a normal woman.

My education, or rather my remembering, began as I boarded the plane and it continued, non-stop, throughout the whole Egyptian journey. This is what Vanda Osmon of *Joy Travel* promised and delivered, as excerpted from her website.

> You will experience and explore the wisdom of the Ancient Ones and attune to our innate connection with the Divine. Our goal and intention is to ignite the spark of Divine Wisdom, Vision, and Purpose that lies within each of us and to realize our divine purpose through deep remembrance of who we really are.
>
> After arriving in Cairo, we will fly to Aswan where we will embark on our five-day Nile Cruise aboard the deluxe MS Liberty Cruise ship, stopping at the temples which symbolically represent the gates to our chakra center within our bodies. At each Temple along the Nile we will meditate and attune to the Temple's wisdom, opening the gifts that each one has to offer us. As we journey we will integrate these wisdoms as we prepare for our private visit within the Great Pyramid of Giza.

For me, this journey was bitter sweet. In each temple we visited, there were flashes of past-life memories. Were they my memories? My ancestors? Or were they holographic scenes recorded in the temples themselves, played back when triggered by one who was open and sensitive to its story? I don't know. There was a sense of familiarity, but not a sense of peace and comfort.

Many times, as I walked through a temple, I was inner-directed to command the downloading of the information held in the hieroglyphs. The temple in Karnack, in particular, contained column after column of hieroglyphs, representing a library of ancient wisdom. As I walked past each column, I felt that I was receiving records that would be available for my conscious mind sometime in the future when I needed it.

Each temple along the Nile represented a particular chakra in the human body and was dedicated to the emotional, mental, physical and spiritual mastery of that chakra. We participated in ancient initiations, igniting the memories and codes that previously lay dormant, waiting for activation. Many times during these initiations, I would feel that I had done this before. A few times I remembered the ancient initiation a little differently, knowing that their modern rendition, while very close, was just a little bit off. Knowing, too, that it didn't matter. All of us who took the initiate's journey needed only to reawaken the memory. We had all mastered these initiations in previous lifetimes.

It was during this time that I became aware of the value of initiation as a tool for expanding consciousness and furthering evolution. Each initiation causes a permanent transformation. Usually delivered with ceremony in an atmosphere of sacred reverence, initiations are energy transmissions from initiator to initiate. They move you from one energetic frequency to a higher one, at the same time expanding your consciousness.

An integration period of at least three days always follows. During this time you will adjust to the energetic difference and expanded consciousness and like a snake, shed the old skin to reveal the fresh new skin underneath. This trip renewed my love for initiations and sacred ceremony.

All went reasonably well until the final leg of the trip when we arrived at the Giza Plateau. I took one look at the Great Pyramid and collapsed in the sand, surrendering to a half hour of violent sobbing. My tour buddies gathered around to console and support me, holding a loving space for me, even though I could not articulate the cause of my suffering. In retrospect, there were a number of things going on and I got my first clue as to what multi-dimensional beings we truly are.

At one level, I was reacting visually to the Giza Plateau. In my genetic memory, the pyramids were surrounded by lush, beautiful gardens. I even had the sense that maybe I designed and built these gardens. In the present day reality, there are no gardens, only sand. My conscious mind already knew this as I had seen pictures of it before. But somehow I kept flashing to the gardens. The difference between what was then and what is now, was devastating.

What made it worse was all the litter that was blowing around. The shame and grief at the lack of respect for the sacredness of this site was more than I could take.

To add insult to injury, there was a three-legged antenna on top of the Great Pyramid. "It should not be there. **It should not be there!!!** Why is it there? Who put that there? Get it off! Can't you all see it should not be there?" Someone inside of me was outraged!

The Great Pyramid, unlike the other two in the same vicinity, has no capstone. The top is a flat square shape. Intuitively I knew that the three-legged artificial structure was compromising the energetic flow of the four-sided pyramid and obstructing its ability to fulfill its purpose. The Great Pyramid felt oppressed and somehow my empathic abilities tuned into it and I felt it in my own emotional body. No wonder I had shut down my emotional body when I was a child. This degree of empathy was debilitating.

There was also some awareness that the antenna was broadcasting the disharmonious energies of chaos, anger and violence. It could be an over-active imagination, adding $2 + 2$ and getting 5, but after spending a few nights in a nearby hotel, many members of the group reported having bizarre war-like dreams that were foreign to their usual experience. Someone had the inspiration to suggest disconnecting the TVs from the cables in the hotel rooms. We all agreed to try it. The violent war dreams stopped. Interesting?

For better or worse, I allowed this antenna to become a source of suffering for me. I wanted it gone and was convinced that its removal would benefit the planet as well. I solicited the help of the Elemental Kingdom (nature spirits of wind, rain, fire and earth) and asked that, "If it be for the highest good of all concerned, please use your power of wind, rain and lightning to remove the antenna. If it is in the highest good of all concerned that the antenna remains, then I surrender to your wisdom."

That night, a thunder and lightning storm surprised everybody, except me. The Egyptians were grateful for the gift of rain, which never falls in March. The tourists were grateful for the incredible light show, including the lightning that hit the antenna on top of the Great Pyramid, but did not knock it off. I was grateful to the Elemental Kingdom for their response to my request. I was glad I had enough humility and compassion to entertain the possibility that maybe my outrage was misplaced and that there was higher wisdom at work. I surrendered to the antenna.

I experienced myself as a powerful, yet humble, Goddess who could invoke the cooperation of Nature. The experience itself was an initiate's practice exercise, calling for the balance of wisdom, power and compassion. Had I stood in anger and arrogance and not allowed for the possibility of higher wisdom, I would have created karma related to abuse of power. As it turned out, the thunderstorm was a gift for everybody.

The next day we were scheduled to go to the Sphinx. Vanda had gotten permission for us to spend one hour between the Sphinx's paws. While still in Sedona, I had felt guided to purchase a particular crystal. Then when I was packing for the trip, I felt guided to pack the crystal. This morning I felt guided to take the crystal with me to the Sphinx. Once between the paws, I asked my Inner Advisors for direction. They said, "Download the Hall of Records into your cells and into the crystal."

Edgar Cayce and others reported that the Hall of Records is under one of the paws of the Sphinx, so the instructions from my advisors were not a big surprise. My Inner Advisors told me that the Hall of Records was a living library for all the universes. It surprised me that I should download the records into my cells. Since then, I have learned that our DNA acts as an incredibly huge storage unit for information. Why I would need the Hall of Records in my DNA is still a mystery. I was also told that someday in the future, I would be directed to give the crystal to a certain individual. Trusting my guidance, I have been a loving caretaker for the crystal.

Our next adventure led us back to the Great Pyramid. Vanda had gotten permission for us to be in the King's Chamber of the Great Pyramid at the moment of Spring Equinox, for an entire hour. Our group of 40 initiates participated in sacred ceremony and toning led by Diana James. There is a sarcophagus in the King's Chamber that has been used for initiations throughout the ages. We each took a turn lying in the sarcophagus for one minute while

Diana toned and sang our name. Again, I was overcome with emotion and just kept repeating the words, "I accept, I accept" over and over again for the entire minute. I had the sense that I was receiving a precious gift. Indeed, this initiation was the culmination of all the initiations, receiving the gift of immortality.

There were additional flashes of memory and understanding. I knew that in my soul's past I had spent lifetimes preparing for this initiation. We had to master our bodies to the degree that we could survive inside a closed sarcophagus for three days while our consciousness left and the cells of the body transmuted themselves while receiving massive energy transmissions from the Heavens.

Let me define immortality as I know it. It isn't necessarily like you become Super Man and can survive a volley of bullets in the chest or that if you were run over by a train, your body would put itself back together. It's more like, you raise your consciousness above mortality. You can decide to live in your body in perfect health, without aging for as long as you choose. You are not vulnerable to disease. And because of your expanded consciousness, you won't be subject to "accidents" because you won't attract them. Whenever you are ready to leave this body, because you don't want it or need it anymore, you can just withdraw your consciousness gracefully and leave the body behind.

Along the same line, if you choose to take another body, here or on some other planet or dimension, you can move into it consciously. You won't be subject to the Veil of Forgetfulness where you forget who you are, where you've been, and what you are there for. It's all about consciousness.

I believe I received the codes for my own immortality that day. There was some rather beautiful and surprising validation when I returned home to Sedona.

Keeping my vow to sit with the Aura Star again, I made an appointment for the next day. I couldn't wait to see what it showed me. This time, my whole aura was a beautiful cobalt blue except for that same violet satellite dish on my head. But now all my chakras had turned white and instead of being circular, they were cubed. The Aura Star operator admitted never seeing this before and she didn't know what it meant.

Later I learned from another teacher that our chakras transform to cube-shaped multi-dimensional tunnels when we receive the gift of immortality. I definitely felt different. I could tell my frequency was higher and my consciousness had expanded yet again. There definitely was a quickening of my psychic gifts. But other than that, I still felt quite human.

I wasn't back in Sedona very long when I started to get the idea that maybe Sedona was finished with me. There was always the awareness that Sedona was a transitional healing place, and not my permanent home. Still, I loved it so. I had made so many friends that felt like my soul family. My healing practice was successful and I adored my beautiful home at the base of Thunder Mountain.

Yet when the signs and signals presented themselves, I knew better than to resist. When Sedona is done with you, you better leave immediately and gracefully. Otherwise you'll be spun out and it's not a pretty sight. I watched enough people resist and the painful dramas their Higher Selves created to force them to leave. Since I had asked to be guided through graceful transitions, I decided to do my part and surrender. I agreed to leave. Even though I suspected that Kaua'i was calling, I stayed open to guidance that might lead me somewhere else.

Around the same time, a couple who were both Feng Shui Masters wanted to experience my clearing sessions and asked if I would be willing to trade for a Feng Shui reading on my house. I was reluctant to do this given that I knew I would be leaving Sedona soon, but they informed me that you Feng Shui for the future. The energy I would set in this home would set the stage and support my next home. I agreed.

This couple had studied a form of Feng Shui that is very precise and mathematical, unlike the "Black Hat" form, which is more intuitive. They prefer to work from the blueprints, but since I was renting, I didn't have them. They came to take measurements and draw up a plan so they could do their calculations. While taking their measurements, they noticed the position of my desk, where I do my writing. They asked about the state of my business and creativity.

The truth was I hadn't been writing at all. I seemed to have writer's block. I was also having trouble with my website. My former web host had skipped town and seemed to have taken my website with him, parking it in cyberspace where I could not access it for updates. I had hired another webmaster to try to get my website back, but despite his efforts over the past few weeks, he still could not gain access to it.

The Feng Shui Masters told me that my desk was in the absolute worst place in the house and that I should just move it "anywhere else" until they could tell me the exact best place for it. Taking their wisdom to heart, as soon as they left, I called a friend to help me move the desk. We had just picked it up off the ground and moved it about six feet when the phone rang. It was my new webmaster telling me he had just gained access to my website. WOW! What immediate confirmation.

We moved the desk to a new location. Within a few days I felt inspired to write an article entitled *Goddess to Warrior: How to Transform the Feminine*. I submitted my article to SpiritWeb, one of the first spiritual websites to publish Spirit-Guided writings. I was overwhelmed by the response. Emails began pouring in from all over the world. It was such a kick to look at my website statistics and see that people from over 50 countries had come to visit my site after reading my article on SpiritWeb. For the first time, I really felt like a citizen of the World. The planet just got smaller.

When the Feng Shui Masters returned with their findings, they told me the best place for the desk. I moved the desk again and this time, the result was even more profound. I wrote *Radiant One* which became the beginning of this book. But before page two was written, a year later, I was launched into the next higher level of frequency and consciousness. Along with that came more incredible journeys and adventures.

My dear friend Madaline had heard my stories about Kaua'i and wanted to go there with me. Patti was also feeling called back to Kaua'i. The three of us planned a trip together. I contacted the family on Kaua'i who had offered to sponsor me there. The last time I had talked to them, they couldn't wait to have me back to continue their inner clearing work. But when I called this time, they let me know they had changed their minds about supporting me.

Although disappointed, my inner guidance told me that since my initiations, my energy had shifted and there would be many who didn't resonate with me anymore. I was told that even though they had expressed their love, support and enthusiasm for my work, they were a "false family" and that a new family that resonated with me at my new frequency would show up.

I was able to set up another radio interview early in my visit, which I felt would draw some clients, if that was part of the Divine Plan. I surrendered to the process and just vowed to enjoy my time with Madaline and Patti and see what Kaua'i had to offer.

My radio interview with Dr. Ann West of *Truth from the Source* went well. I forgot to ask her to record the interview, so on the way out the studio door, I put out a little prayer, that someone out there had taped it and would contact me with a copy.

The prayer was answered a couple of days later when I got a call from Kathy Russell. She said that a friend of hers had felt guided by his spirit to tape my radio interview and give it to her. Kathy had the copy of my interview that I had prayed for.

In addition, her guides were telling her that we should meet and that there was more to share with me. I could feel a spirit-led adventure brewing, so I agreed immediately to meet them at the site of a new home they were building. When I arrived, I was greeted warmly by two jovial beings, Kathy and Rod Russell — a trance-channel team. Rod is the trance-channel who has the ability to go into a trance and allow spirit to come into his body and speak through him. Kathy is a conscious channel, which means she hears spirit speaking and relays the messages while still remaining conscious in her body. Kathy acts as a guide and protector for Rod when he leaves his body in a trance state.

The couple delighted me with stories of how Spirit had led them from Santa Rosa, CA to Kaua'i to build this house. They were told that the house wasn't just for them — it was to be shared. At that point only the foundation and floor boards were in place. They painted a picture of how it would look when it was done.

They also told me that Rod had channeled a being called Enoch who had a few good things to say about me. I had read The Keys of Enoch by J.J. Hurtak, so I was familiar with the name. They were guided to offer me support in the way of introducing me and my work to their network. It seemed evident that this was the "true" family that Spirit had told me would show up. I told my friends Madaline and Patti about them and we all decided to book a joint channeling session.

Merlin showed up to speak to us through Rod. The information and energy he brought through was very supportive. Both Patti and I were told that we would be very supported if we decided to make our new home on Kaua'i. I fell in love with this couple, who felt like Mr. and Mrs. Santa Claus to me. Kaua'i was starting to feel more and more like home.

Meanwhile, Madaline, Patti and I enjoyed our time together — spending lots of time at the beach. One afternoon after returning to our car, Patti and I found the window broken and our purses gone. While I had only a few dollars in my purse, Patti had over $600 that she had saved for months to use on this trip. It was the second time in a year that my wallet was stolen. We were informed, too late, that rental cars parked at remote locations were often targets for this kind of theft. It's better to take your valuables with you and leave the door unlocked.

Despite this setback, Patti announced that she had decided she was going to make Kaua'i her home. At that point, I was seriously entertaining the idea, but not ready to commit. Madaline was clear that Sedona was still her home. Yet, being on this island rekindled her desire to go to the Greek Islands. She asked me if I wanted to go with her. Every cell of my body yelled "YES" and the word blurted out of my mouth before I could stop it.

Europe Calls

Patti went back to Michigan to begin wrapping things up there for her move to Kaua'i. Madaline and I went back to Sedona and began talking about our upcoming trip to Greece. After being gone for three weeks, I found that the article posted on SpiritWeb had found many new readers and people interested in my clearing sessions. Most of the interest came from Europe. Two women, one in Zurich, Switzerland and one in Istanbul, Turkey wanted to come to Sedona to work exclusively with me. When I mentioned that I was going to Greece, the one in Zurich jumped at the chance to meet me in there instead. The woman from Istanbul offered to sponsor a workshop for me in her home.

One of my Sedona clients had a friend in Austria who she felt would be interested in my work. Sure enough, the friend offered to sponsor a workshop in Graz. A European Tour started taking shape quite effortlessly. A friend, Shery, from Sedona told me that chances were pretty good she would be going to Valencia, Spain around the same time and wouldn't it be fun to meet there? Of course it would! Spain was added to the tour, just like that.

Diana James, who I went to Egypt with, told me that she had gotten instructions from her Spirit Guides to go to France and anchor the *Sacred Union* energy into the planet. She was told there were several other women who would feel called to join her and that she should "Follow the Mystery of the Dove." The words "*Sacred Union*" resonated with me at such a deep, deep level. I wasn't even sure what it was all about, but I knew I wanted to be part of it. France was added to the tour.

I was excited to share with Madaline how our planned trip to Greece, was expanding into a real European adventure. To my surprise, she informed me that after further contemplation, she couldn't really afford to go on another trip so soon. She wasn't going to Greece with me after all.

This was a shock, yet there was an inner knowing that Madaline had served as the catalyst to get me to take this trip. Instead of being angry or hurt, I was grateful to her for playing her part so well. Likewise, Shery bowed out of the trip to Spain, but because that was in between a workshop commitment in Istanbul and my *Sacred Union* commitment in France, I decided to keep it on the schedule and go there myself. Had it not been for Shery, I would have already booked my flight home instead of being available for Diana's invitation.

Answering the Call

Plans for the European Adventure fell into place so easily, I knew I was on the right path and everything was in Divine Right Order. Even as I made the plans, the knowing became stronger that my time in Sedona was drawing to a close. So I spent as much time with the red rocks as I could.

One day while meditating outside on a big red rock at the base of Cathedral Hill, Mother Earth spoke to me. I saw a swirling tornado-like vortex that started at my waist and went all the way into the core of the Earth. Intuitively I knew this image represented my connection to Mother Earth through Sedona. Suddenly I saw the tip of the vortex disconnect from the core of the Earth and come quickly spiraling back, slamming into my solar plexus with tremendous force. Sedona and I were complete with each other. Grief flooded my heart and tears spilled from my eyes.

The grief lasted for a few days and I didn't resist it. I allowed myself to feel in full strength, expressing it through crying and dancing. As the grief subsided, images of Kaua'i, the beautiful Garden Isle, presented themselves for my comfort.

A phone call to Kathy and Rod on Kaua'i confirmed my suspicions that Kaua'i was my new home. The loving couple invited me to live in the guest room of their new home, scheduled to be completed by October. So the plan was, pack and leave Sedona by the end of September, tour Europe during October and November and move to Kaua'i on December 1. With that settled, I began dismantling my home in Sedona.

European Adventure

Greece

Athens, Greece was the first stop on my tour. I met Esther from Zurich there and we spent 11 days touring three of the Greek Islands: Crete, Santorini and Mykonos. As we toured, I moved Esther through the clearing sessions, one every other day, giving her time to integrate in between. By the end of her tour, she had completed the entire clearing program that I was offering at that time. Even after the first session, clearing male and female issues, I could see some results. She looked softer, more open and more feminine. She bought some new clothes that reflected the Goddess that was emerging from within.

Based on her subsequent emails to me over the next few months, the work we did together propelled her into a whole new expression. She lost weight, changed her wardrobe to a more feminine appearance, began offering healing classes at the insurance company she worked for and met the man of her dreams. She was deliciously happy in her new life.

After Esther left, I stayed on the island of Mykonos for another week by myself. Alone, in a foreign country, facing two months of traveling by myself, no place that I could really call home, I plunged into a deep depression. Self-doubt overtook me as I questioned why I was, once again, giving up everything that I loved just because of little voices I heard in my head. Was I going crazy? I began to think so.

I had hoped to make friends easily on Mykonos, which is known as the party capital of the Mediterranean. But it was mid-October and the tourists and the parties were thinning. I walked around the town in a daze, feeling invisible, not connecting with anybody. All the while, I held my composure as best I could, even while feeling like bursting into tears at any moment. Self-doubt and self-pity had their way with me for several days. Somewhere inside me, I knew I was going through the "Dark Night of the Soul."

Finally I reached out for help and phoned a massage therapist that practiced Reiki. She had a loving maternal presence and I allowed myself to be comforted. After asking me a few questions and realizing that I myself was a healing facilitator, she asked me what advice I would give a client who was in my position. Of course, the first thing I always do is go within for guidance. I was told, "Listen to your tapes." Of course, it was so easy. Why didn't I think of that?

For some, I am told, the "Dark Night of the Soul" can last weeks or even years. For me, the tapes moved me through this transition in one and a half hours. First, I listened to the tape that I had recorded, and sold to all my clients, called Activation Station. This guided meditation tape clears the energy system of stagnant energy. It uses the energy of the "Triple Flame" to clear and balance the chakras and clear the meridian energy pathways. The Triple Flame energy is a very potent blend of Divine Love, Divine Wisdom and Divine Power. It is the energy that Jesus used and initiated the Apostles with. Jesus and the Apostles used the Triple Flame energy for the healing miracles they performed.

I followed that tape up with the *Integration Station* tape. This guided visualization calls in higher frequencies of light, one by one, giving them a chance to wash through the four-body system and raise the frequency and expand the consciousness. Using the two tapes together was a powerful double-whammy that kicked me out of depression and into a pleasant, blissful state of contentment.

Feeling invisible only hours before, now when I walked down the street, everyone greeted me. They commented on my outfit, my smile, the weather, asked for directions — anything to connect. What a difference! Feeling a new sense of wonder and curiosity, I decided to take an excursion to a nearby island — Delos.

Delos was, according to mythology, the birth-place of the twins Apollo and Artemis, offspring of Zeus and Leto. Hera, Zeus' sister and wife, chased Leto to the ends of the world for having an affair with her husband. Being the goddess of motherhood, Hera refused to help Leto in childbirth, causing her to suffer through nine days of labor before giving birth to Artemis and four days later to Apollo. The island itself, once hidden, came to the surface and kept moving around the Aegean Sea thus avoiding Hera's vengeance.

Delos became known as a sacred place with splendid buildings and sanctuaries.

The island itself is relatively small — but it is monumental in Greek history and mythology. Delos is not only the geological center of the Cyclades, but was once the commercial, religious, and commercial center. Because it was considered sacred, over the centuries, many different religions built temples there and the spiritual communities coexisted peacefully.

Today Delos is essentially a large archeological site with no inhabitants except members of The French School of Archeology, who have been excavating the island for over 100 years. It seems like every square foot has some kind of ruins or artifacts.

Oddly, it was a temple face at the top of a hill that drew my immediate and focused attention. I say temple face, because that was all that was left standing amongst the ruins. The tour guide told me that the object of my affection was a Temple to the Goddess Isis. That's all I needed to hear and I was off and running up the hill to meet her.

Just beyond the entrance to the temple, stood a large statue of Isis — headless, of course. I stood at her feet and presented myself as a long-lost daughter, happy to return to the arms of her mother. There had been so many past-life memories related to the Daughters of Isis cult, in Egypt, Rome and now Greece. I imagined I felt her welcome, yet at the same time, heard her scolding, telling me that it was time I let go of the daughter stuff and step into the Isis energy myself.

Glad to be alone, I straightened my stance and surrendered to the gifts of Isis. Waves of energy moved through me, accompanied by scenes from the past, and the 'knowing' that I had lived here before. It took a while to adjust to the Isis energy; yet once I did, it seemed like a very familiar flavor. Giving thanks, I said goodbye and went to look for my old room in the temple.

I wandered around the ruins of the temple, nothing really feeling familiar. The ferry tooted its horn, signaling the tourists to return to the docks. Disappointed, I started in the direction of the ferry. On the way, I found a room that I hadn't seen before. Suddenly memories flooded back and I recognized the mosaic pattern on the floor. My room! Yes, of course it would be facing the ocean. A room with a view — how me!

Lost in memories, the second sounding of the horn brought me back to the present. I hurried down the hill, concerned that the distance between me and the dock might be too great to get there in time. Gravity helped a swift decline.

Self-doubt raised its ugly head and argued that, once again, my imagination was getting away with me. How could I believe that the statue talked to me, gave me an energy transmission and then flooded me with memories? The Goddess in my heart and ego in my mind were battling for position. Not knowing who to believe, I sent out a prayer to Isis, "If this is really my old neighborhood, give me a sign."

I soon found myself walking alongside other tourists, overhearing a 'getting acquainted' conversation between a married couple and two men. "Where are you from?" "Michigan," was the response. "I'm from Michigan too," I interjected. All eyes turned toward me. We discovered that the woman and I grew up two streets away from each other — in the same neighborhood. We even went to the same private high school, which wasn't in the neighborhood. How's that for confirmation?

Her husband asked me, "Did you feel something special in that temple?" I said that I imagined that I had lived there before in another lifetime. He elbowed his wife and said, "See, I told you." Somehow, he had the intuition that both he and I had lived there before. Needless to say, we all bonded quickly and enjoyed each other's company for the next few days.

October's air was growing colder and the wind blowing harder, making Mykonos much less attractive. The sea was too rough to travel by boat to any other islands, so I moved over to the sunnier, less windy side of the island for the last few days of my Greek tour. The resort was beautiful, white-washed with bougainvillea in bloom all around. Yet, tourist season was coming to the end and they were preparing to close the resort. Next stop — Istanbul.

Istanbul

My hostess, Zeynep, met me at the airport and took me to the tourist section of town for something to eat and to get acquainted. Istanbul, which used to be called Constantinople, is where East meets West. There are two distinct cultures: European representing the West and Asian, representing the East. Zeynep lived on the Asian side of town. I was amazed at how soon we felt comfortable with each other.

It was Zeynep's dream to start a healing center where she could host teachers and healers from all over the world. She didn't have a place yet, so hosting me in her living room was her first step in the direction of her dreams. She put together a small group of women, most of whom could speak English, except one, who only spoke Turkish and Star Language. Zeynep would have to translate for her.

Zeynep told me that part of the Turkish cultural mentality was to be very skeptical and distrusting. She suggested that I find a way to establish credibility with these women right away or they would be likely to just get up and leave. Oh great! How do I do that?

By now, surrender had been an almost moment-to-moment exercise. I sent out a quick prayer for help in establishing credibility quickly. Zeynep introduced me to the group, we greeted each other and then I attempted to launch into my standard presentation.

My own curiosity distracted me. Fascinated by the idea of 'Star Language' I requested to hear some. The woman seemed delighted to be invited to speak. She talked to the group in what sounded like a somewhat childish, musical version of Hebrew or Sanskrit. After delivering her address in Star Language, she translated it into Turkish for the group. Finally, Zeynep translated it into English for me.

She told the group that they were very lucky to have me here and that I was bringing information from very far away. She said that I would be writing a book on something completely new and would be back in Istanbul to teach again sometime in the future. They paid close attention and participated fully in the workshop. Zeynep was pleased that they seemed to be very impressed and the women reported some profound shifts and releases during the workshop.

A week after I left, I got an email from Zeynep saying that her healing center had magically materialized. A house she inherited, which she was renting out under a year's lease, suddenly became vacant. It was in a perfect location for a healing center. She was ecstatic and felt that the healing she had done on her mother/father issues during my workshop had opened the way for this great opportunity much sooner than she had thought possible.

Austria

Next stop, Graz, Austria. I flew from Istanbul to Vienna and took a train from Vienna to Graz. Judith, my sponsor, met me at the train station and drove me to her apartment where she lived with her 11-year-old son. She had registered 14 participants for the workshop, both men and women. Up until now, mostly women had been attracted to the work through the *Warrior to Goddess, How To Transform the Feminine* article that had appeared on *SpiritWeb*. In fact, the name of this workshop was *Transforming the Feminine*, so I was surprised to have a male doctor, teacher and policeman attend. Yet, they seemed open and happy to be there, so I said a prayer of gratitude and went with the flow.

Judith and two other women took turns translating my English to German. I wore my personal harmonizer pendant, which is a sound-activated energy tool developed by Slim Spurling for teachers. Besides harmonizing your personal energy field, it transmits your message 12 levels deep. It must have worked well because half-way through the workshop, the participants told the interpreters to stop; they could understand me without interpretation.

Typically when I present this workshop, I like to take the group out for a little devic communication. Devas are the organizing and maintaining consciousness that is attached to all form. Everything in form has a deva who is in charge of holding that form or energetic blueprint in the physical world. Everything is energy; the energy of love. All of creation is just pure love energy. A creator God applies intention to the love energy to create. The Creator, commanding, "I create a tree" sets the intention, which holds the consciousness and organizing blueprint of tree. Every species of tree has an over-lighting deva of the species, and every individual tree has its own deva.

All indigenous people knew this and communicated with the nature and elemental devas. The relationship between deva and human is that the human gives the instructions and the devas carry them out. With the rise of the patriarchal systems, the rise of science and the value given only to that which you can observe and measure, most people on the planet have forgotten this.

The native Hawaiians remember and perhaps that is one reason the islands feel so alive. The nature spirits are still honored in song, dance and ceremony.

I asked the group in Austria if they had a sacred place or a power spot nearby where we could take a field trip. One woman said that they did have a place that used to be a power spot, but it had been altered and she and some of the other participants hoped that we could do a clearing on the land. Tickled that we had a mission, I agreed and we planned to meet at the site the next morning at 10 a.m.

That evening, I tuned into the site to see if I could intuitively pick up information on what was going on there. To my amazement, I saw that there was an intersection of ley lines and a big vortex that had been programmed with judgment, hatred and fear. I saw the devas of the region had been enslaved to carry forward this program and they were suffering greatly, as this type of de-evolutionary program was alien to their nature. A voice inside me said, "This is clearly the work of Hitler." I remember reading that Hitler was very much interested in the ley lines of the Earth and in the occult. It seemed that he had programmed the vortex to broadcast an illusionary matrix that supported his beliefs and mission. Even though the war had been over for decades, the program was still running.

Later I learned that there was a huge resurgence of pro-Nazi sentiment among the 20 to 30 year old men in Austria. This was baffling as this generation had not been exposed to these philosophies through the educational system and their parents were not supportive of these views. It was something that was "unmentionable" in almost all circles. Could it be that the vortices programmed generations ago were still operating?

Admittedly, I felt more than a bit intimidated at the thought of going against Hitler in this way. I prayed for guidance and reassurance and was told I would not have been given the assignment had I not been ready and able to handle it with the help of my group. Willingness and openness was all that was called for. Having plenty of both, I charged ahead.

The next morning brought torrential rain, which had not been forecast. The participants were phoning the house asking if our field trip was still on. They were told to bring umbrellas and boots and meet as planned.

Connecting with the nature elementals, I told them of our intention to restore freedom to this sacred site and asked for their cooperation and support. Their response was to stop the rain, timed perfectly with our arrival at the site.

The site was in a public park overlooking the city. I connected with Gertrude, the woman who had originally suggested this site and asked, "Who altered the energy of this place?" She diverted her eyes and shyly said, "Hitler," confirming my suspicions. Gertrude said that she always asked the teachers and healers who came through town to work on this spot. So far the results were negligible. I told her I couldn't promise anything, but was willing to give it my best shot.

Diana James, my friend and teacher, had taught me geobiology (healing sick energy in the Earth) and devic communication. I passed along what I had learned to this group. Gertrude volunteered to be interpreter for the devas since she had developed the ability to communicate with them quite clearly.

We got in a circle and did an opening ceremony, stating our intention to be of loving and supportive service to the Divine Plan, the Earth, this property and the devas who served it. We did a sacred temple dance and offered the energy to the devas. The group offered individual gifts that they had intuitively felt called to bring. We gave the command to free the devas from the previous instructions and align themselves with the new intention of Mother Earth to ascend. Then I instructed Gertrude to ask the devas what more they requested from us to help them heal and carry out the new plan. Gertrude said they asked for "more light."

We held hands in a circle and I invoked the light, imagining it coming from Heaven into the Earth through our circle. Immediately, a hole in the clouds appeared directly above our circle and sunshine poured through. We all burst into joyous tears at this beautiful validation of our love and intention. Gertrude said that the devas were dancing and celebrating. I turned up the music on the portable CD player and the group joined in the celebration with the devas.

With their attention diverted into ecstatic dance, I silently asked if there were any further instructions from my spiritual team. They told me to anchor the Platinum Ray into this land. The Platinum Ray comes from the Great Central Moon in the Great Central Universe and is the energy of the Divine Feminine Aspect of Source. Before humans, like me, began anchoring it into the land, only the dolphins and whales held this energy in the oceans.

This Divine Feminine energy would begin to restore male/female balance and begin to heal our world, and give the feminine the support, courage, safety and nourishment to stand equal to men. It seemed that Spirit gave me instructions to anchor that energy, pretty much everywhere I went.

I imagined my body as an acupuncture needle in the Earth, allowing the Platinum Ray to flow into the top of my head, all the way through my body and into the core of the Earth. Allowing this energy to wash through me for a few minutes, I stood still, with my eyes closed and my faced tilted toward the sky.

When I opened my eyes, Gertrude and her daughter were waiting silently to talk to me. Gertrude's daughter was very excited about dolphins and whales and wanted to share with me how much she loved them. I chuckled, knowing that Spirit had just sent me validation that the Platinum Ray had been successfully anchored. The women felt the energy and that was what inspired their talk of dolphins and whales in the middle of the Austrian countryside.

The workshop concluded later that afternoon with many tears of joy and appreciation flowing freely. I spent the next few days with Judith as she showed me the beautiful Austrian landscape. It was late October and the leaves were in full color, rolling, like waves, along the hilly terrain.

On Sunday we visited grape country and sampled the new wine, fine cheeses and sausages. The whole day seemed like something out of a story book. My eyes were caressed by one postcard view after another. I enjoyed my time with Judith, knowing that the next week I would be traveling alone again, in yet another foreign country, not knowing the language.

Spain

Spain had called, and I responded. I had been to Barcelona before and loved their aquarium. The rest of the city, with so many people and buildings, seemed like just another big city to me.

It was becoming clear that my sensitivity to energy had increased dramatically and it was getting difficult to me to be around a lot of people or buildings that held a lot of energetic memory. Clearly, I was more comfortable in small, low density towns. Concrete absorbed some of the dense energy, yet it ricocheted the excess between the city buildings until I felt it was coming at me from all directions. Not sure how far my workshop receipts would stretch, I decided to stay in some low-budget hotels in the city. Big mistake!

Within two days over arriving Barcelona, after witnessing a purse snatching on the street, I was ready for something smaller. Nothing about this city seemed familiar or supportive; just another big city. Yet I was beginning to understand what kind of environments nourished me.

When I choose a hotel only because it had a good price, I felt miserable. When I paid more to stay in a place that seemed nurturing, I flourished. The difference in price wasn't really that much, but the difference in my sense of well-being was huge.

At one point, I felt so miserable, I sent out an angry ultimatum to my spirit guides. "I've found a flight to LAX for $500 and I'm going to take it tomorrow and skip the whole France thing unless you find me a nurturing place to stay. I want beauty. I want it to be affordable and comfortable. I want it to be easy. And I want companionship with somebody who is spiritual, knows the area, speaks English and can show me the sights." Then I walked into a travel agency with a poster for a flight directly to LAX for $500.

I inquired about the flight to LAX, which was open and immediately available. Then, I made another inquiry. I asked, "Is there anywhere around here that is considered a spiritual or healing place? Somewhere away from a big city, maybe a small beautiful bed and breakfast near the ocean?"

The travel agent informed me that she only handled big hotels, but the Tourist Board, just around the corner, had lists of smaller hotels. The tourist board found me a beautiful spot at the eastern tip of Spain called Javea, a popular spa destination because of the healing qualities of the water there.

It turned out to be easy to catch a bus to Javea and I was soon happily on my way, feeling that, once again, Spirit had answered my prayer. I arrived in the downtown district across from what, I thought, was a taxi stand. After waiting for a half hour for a taxi to come by, I finally asked a gentleman who was passing by if the sign with the big "T" on it overlooking the word TAXI painted on the curb was a taxi stand after all.

He explained that the space was reserved for a taxi if one were to call on the telephone and hire one. But official taxi stand was at the top of the hill. As my eyes took in the steep incline of the hill I would have to negotiate with my luggage, I imagine he took pity on me. He asked my destination and then offered to give me a ride to my hotel.

Normally I wouldn't advise getting in a car with a stranger, but a quick check with my inner guides told me he was safe. Not only was the gentleman safe, but he proved to be the companion I had prayed for, and for the next few days he showed me the sights in and around Javea. It seemed that, I too, had been an answer to his prayers. He said he felt inspired by the stories of my spiritual quest and happy to learn that there were some women in the world who could be kind without being manipulative and controlling. He said he wanted to prepare himself to open his heart to an intimate relationship. In gratitude for his time and kindness, I gifted him with a clearing session to help him release his blocks around female relationships.

The small hotel in Javea was lovely and filled with Swiss, German and English tourists. I spent five days there, mostly resting and preparing for my next big adventure in France.

France

In November 2000, Diana was directed by her spiritual guides to go to France and anchor the *Sacred Union* energy into the planet. She was told to "follow the Mystery of the Dove." Very cryptic instructions indeed, but somehow the sound of this mission resonated, at a deep soul level, with me and four other women. We decided to make this journey together and see what adventures awaited us as we let spirit guide our way. Investing our own time, energy and money, we commenced this sacred mission in joyful service to the planet.

Led by Diana James and Vanda Osmon of *Joy Travel, Inc.*, we experienced many magical, mystical adventures. The link between *Sacred Union* energy and *The Mystery of the Dove* seemed to center around the sacred sites visited by Mary Magdalene when she relocated to the South of France where she lived as a spiritual teacher and healer until the end of her days.

It is suggested that Jesus and the Magdalene were Divine Compliments, both having studied in mystery schools around the world, and receiving initiations into their Divine, Immortal and Ascended states of consciousness. They were equal partners, with equally powerful, yet different and complimentary metaphysical gifts — grounding the Divine Masculine and Divine Feminine into human bodies. Could it be that this couple embodied the *Sacred Union* of Spirit and Human that was to be a model for the world? Was their mission to remind us of our own Divine nature?

The world was not quite ready to embrace this teaching. Instead of being seen as Jesus' Divine Compliment and partner, the Magdalene was characterized as a prostitute. The women of the bible were portrayed as crones, virgins or whores. Obviously, sexuality was discouraged. Disempowering that potent creative energy effectively dismantled the path of enlightenment through sacred sexuality, which until that point in history, had been a timed-honored path.

What did all this have to do with me? In the past 25 years, I had been on my own spiritual quest. I had studied many of the teachings of the mystery schools and received many of the same initiations in sacred temples around the world. For the past three years, I practiced *Integrative Natural Healing*, a spiritual technology that effectively removed stored emotional energy, limiting beliefs and thought patterns from my system. With focused attention, I called on the energy of grace and help from the Spirit realm and let go of my mind-created image of myself. I purified my emotional, mental and spiritual body.

Throwing off the self-imposed shackles of my past, I claimed my right to express myself fully in each moment. I gave myself the freedom to live from my heart and share my love and joy as I pleased. I felt my own Divine nature drawing ever more close to me. At times, I felt like a fountain overflowing with joy and love. But alas, the spray of the fountain evaporated quickly, disappearing swiftly, with no one close by to witness or be nourished by it. I yearned for a playmate whose own light would compliment mine, and one who's loving attention would nurture me into even more full-bodied radiance.

That's why anchoring *Sacred Union* energy onto the planet with Diana and the other women appealed to me. I reasoned that if I allowed my body to act as a lightning rod, grounding the *Sacred Union* energy into the Earth, then it would somehow make me a magnet for a *Sacred Union Partner* in my own life.

Our first adventure in France led us to the cathedral in Chartres. Under the cathedral there is an ancient Druid labyrinth. The labyrinth has been re-created on the floor of the cathedral. The builders of this cathedral employed Sacred Geometry in its structure with the intent that just being in the building would raise your frequency. It was in this cathedral that we were invited to partake of the Catholic Mass. I had grown up Catholic, but had since left the Church and its seemingly vacant rituals. On this day, for some reason, taking Mass in this sacred place appealed to all of us.

Even though the Mass was said in French, the ritual was more alive for me than at any other time in my life. Finally, I got it — I was receiving the Body of Christ. My body and energy system, that I had spent so much time purifying, was the Bride and the Christ Consciousness was the Bridegroom. The male aspect of the Christ Consciousness was anchored into my body that day. There was another immaculate conception, as I was seeded with the desire to teach *Sacred Union*. And of course, in order to teach it, I had to experience it first. The blueprint, which resided in the sixth dimension, was downloaded to me in the moment I received communion. The ecstasy that ran through my body was electrifying.

Chartres was the first Cathedral we visited, and the "Mystery of the Dove" started to reveal itself. All of the cathedrals we visited paid tribute to the Black Madonna. Some say that the statues of the Black Madonna honor Mary Magdalene as the beloved of Jesus, with the black skin distinguishing and portraying the mysterious difference between her and Mary, the mother of Jesus. Others say that she may have been of Ethiopian descent. The cathedrals were linked together in some kind of pilgrimage network that was being celebrated that year (2000). The logo for this network was a dove.

In Rennes Le Chateau, one of the women in our group found a postcard with a black background and a white dove in the middle. Upon closer investigation, and some rudimentary French translation, we found out that the black background was actually a large rock with a dove-shaped hole in it. When the sun hit the rock at a certain angle, the dove was illuminated. The postcard said something along the lines, "to receive Spirit, be the empty space through which light shines through." Thus we unraveled the Mystery of the Dove. It was as I had experienced: empty yourself of the limitations of the past and make space for Christ Consciousness to enter.

The mystical, magical adventures with Diana and the group continued until we said goodbye after ten wonderful days. With my European tour complete, I looked forward to going back to Kaua'i, this time for good.

Coming Home to Kaua'i

The original plan was to move into Kathy and Rod's guest room until I found a place of my own. But a quick phone call to the couple revealed that their new house was not even close to completion. Arriving in Kaua'i, with no place to live and pregnant with the seed of *Sacred Union*, again I wondered if I had gone crazy.

The rental market in Kaua'i was extremely tight. Real estate investors prefer to market their houses as vacation rentals rather than long-term homes, because it is more lucrative. I found that no matter what I could afford to pay, permanent housing was unavailable. I found a series of temporary housing situations, making it necessary to move frequently. For a person with four planets in the sign of Cancer, this was very unsettling. Especially since I had just come from a two-month tour of Europe, living out of a suitcase for the entire time.

Remembering the promise made to me by the island, I went back to Crater Hill to speak to the island and let it know what I wanted to manifest. I clearly described my desire to manifest a home, a *Sacred Union Partner*, and a way to serve the Light and the planet in joy.

I thought that I should reestablish my healing practice and generate some income. But during the first eight months in Kaua'i, whenever I went inside and asked for spiritual guidance, I was told to "be easy with yourself, don't work, rest, something new is getting ready to be born." I spent a lot of time at the beach and out in nature. I attended every spiritual gathering, networking whenever possible. Of course, I always had one eye open for my *Sacred Union Partner*.

During this time, I did have relationships with two men who I thought might be candidates for *Sacred Union*. Neither relationship lasted very long, but both brought me great gifts. These men mirrored attitudes about intimate relationships that I needed to see and release to be ready for my *Sacred Union Partner*.

Sacred Union: A Journey To Joyful Living

The first one triggered all of the ways my parents attempted to limit and control my natural emotional and creative expressions. Growing up I felt that I had no choice but to suppress my natural exuberance, joy and affection as well as anger, rage and sadness because they were not comfortable with these extreme expressions. My perception was that I was punished when I expressed my emotions. The emotional suppression built up over the years and led me to feel trapped, suffocated and dying inside. Seeing this reflected in my new relationship, I broke free from this pattern. I finally loved myself enough to decide that if this man wasn't comfortable with all of me, then he wasn't what I wanted.

In the second relationship I was confronted with my pattern to attract and be attracted to men who were addicted to alcohol. I faced my issues of fear of intimacy and co-dependent beliefs that my love could "save" him. An even bigger gift came from this relationship. Still believing I could "save" him from himself, I asked Spirit for a way to energetically clear addictions. What was born from that request was much bigger than I ever dreamed possible.

Spirit guided me to read certain books that launched me into an intensive research period. I read books on addictions, DNA and genetics, quantum physics, holographic reality theory and intimate relationships.

All of a sudden, everything clicked into place. I saw the nature of how we create and interact with our reality. I saw an image of a movie projector. There is a light bulb that shines through the film and the projector casts the image onto the screen. In a similar manner, each of us is an individualized aspect of God/Spirit, and this is the light source. Our DNA is the film. Our brain is the projector that creates a holographic projection, which is what we perceive as reality. Everything that we perceive as "real" in the physical world is really a holographic image, including our bodies, other people and all form in the third dimension. The movie "Matrix" suggested this holographic theory and is truer than any of us want to believe.

Take this analogy a step further. As in a movie projector, anything on the film will be projected unto the screen. Likewise, you cannot possibly project anything unto the screen that isn't already in the film. All of the surprising and even uncomfortable situations that we experience in our lives must exist in the film (our DNA).

What is DNA then? It's information, records and data — a huge storage unit for the mind and more. The DNA contains the blueprint for your physical body. It stores information about all of your life experiences including emotions, thoughts and thought patterns, judgments, belief systems and your self-image. Your DNA contains the records for your life's purpose. It contains the blueprint for your Divine Body, which is impervious to aging or disease.

Geneticists have found what they refer to as "junk DNA." This is genetic material that does not seem to be activated at the moment and they can't figure out its purpose. But this DNA is not junk, it is information. These are strands of DNA that when hooked up and activated, give us abilities considered metaphysical. These abilities include extrasensory perception, rejuvenation, immortality, telepathy, psycho kinesis, accessing information and communication from other dimensions, teleportation, bi-location and instant manifestation.

Many people already have some of their 12 strands hooked up and operating to varying degrees. In the past we viewed them as freaks and outcasts. In recent years we view these abilities as spiritual gifts given to only a few blessed people. They are the same abilities attributed to the gods and goddesses of ancient myth.

What if these mythical figures were real beings? Perhaps they are our ancient ancestors from another place or dimension. Maybe they had all 12 strands of DNA connected and ignited and they looked like gods to us. Perhaps somehow in our history the DNA was disconnected or scrambled. Can this extra DNA be reconnected and activated? I was beginning to suspect that it could.

Just after digesting all of this information, my guides gave me another shocking jolt of information. The DNA is **changeable**. That's right! It's just information — data, a story, a script. The script can be rewritten. A new script can be overlaid on top of the old one. When you change the script on the film, you change the holographic images being projected — thus you can change your reality.

How does all this information relate to my request to learn how to clear addictions? Well, what if you could go back and rewrite the script for your life. What if you went back to before your parents conceived you? What if a miracle happened to your parents and they released all of their limiting thoughts, beliefs and stored emotional energy? What if their 12 strands of DNA were fully hooked up and activated? What if without all of their stored judgments, fears, limiting beliefs and thought patterns, they were *Divine Humans*? What if they consciously conceived you in love and joy? What if they didn't have all of their neurosis to project upon you? What if they welcomed you into the world and raised you in an atmosphere of unconditional love? What if you were encouraged to fully express yourself? What if they taught you how to use your God-like powers to manifest your own version of Paradise on Earth and express your unique gifts in joyful service?

Well then, you would not have experienced those situations that closed you down to love and life. You wouldn't have any reason to create those addictions, which numb and distract you from your reality. Having grown up in an environment of unconditional love, you would love and honor yourself. You wouldn't even think of engaging in self-destructive behavior. You'd be living like a God or Goddess in Heaven. Why would you want to alter you consciousness in that scenario?

Then I realized that the ramifications of this went way beyond just clearing addictions. If we grew up with Divine Parents in unconditional love with full expression of Who We Really Are, then we would not create the conditions that lead to disease. We would not have co-dependent, dysfunctional relationships. If everyone were expressing their Divinity, there would be abundance for all. No poverty, no war, no disease. Truly — Paradise on Earth.

Well I found this all very exciting, but the next question was, "How can I change the DNA?" The answer to this question became *The Sacred Union* technology. This is a spiritual technology that was downloaded to me in the same manner in which all inventors and scientists are inspired with new discoveries. The *Sacred Union* technology was born nine months, to the day, from when I was seeded with the desire to teach it, while receiving communion in France.

Much to my dismay, I found that *Sacred Union* is not about relationships outside of yourself. *Sacred Union* is about reuniting all aspects of you, within yourself. It is about reuniting with both the male and female aspects of God and your own inner male and female. It's about reuniting your Spirit with your Ego. It is about reuniting your Divinity with your physical body. When this happens, you may want to draw to yourself an intimate partner to enjoy the outward expression of your inner unity. And then again, you may not.

By definition every human is Divine. The human being is the *Sacred Union* of the individualized consciousness of All That Is and physical matter. Humans are the *Sacred Union* of Spirit and Earth. Yet there are varying degrees to which people are aware of their own Divine nature. There are varying degrees to which people express their Divinity.

As our individual consciousness journeyed into the density of matter, we have felt disconnected from our spiritual Source. We have fallen asleep and dreamed that we are separate from our own Divinity. The process used in the *Sacred Union Program* is a spiritual technology that helps us to awaken and clear away the dream of separation. We rebirth ourselves into the world of form, with the awakened knowing that we are *Divine Human*s creating Paradise on Earth. This program is evolving and currently has four steps:

1. *Sacred Union* of Inner Male and Inner Female

2. *Sacred Union* of Ego and Spirit

3. Birthing the *Divine Human*

4. *Sacred Union* Relationships

Birthing the Divine Human process is in alignment with the Earth Mother as she is ascending, birthing herself into the fifth dimension and shifting from a fear-based reality to a joy-based reality. As more humans express their Divinity, we will see the *Divine Human*s coming together in *Sacred Union* relationships and partnerships. First things, first. Start with the *Sacred Union* within you.

To prepare for the *Divine Birth*, you must first clear the past perceptions and stored emotional energy related to the fear-based reality that supports the Illusion of Separation from Source. The first two steps facilitate this release. The third step starts bringing in the various levels of your own Divinity. Once you are expressing 'Who You Really Are' as a *Divine Human*, you may want move on to the fourth step and manifest an intimate partnership with another *Divine Human*. Or you may want to form *Sacred Union Partnerships* for creative expression or joyful service to the planet.

The *Sacred Union Program* technology is now ready to be shared with those who are ready, willing and able to commit to the changes necessary to align with their own Divinity. It is an accelerated transformational process. If you feel ready to commit to this process, strap on your seatbelt, because your life will change. Please, for your own comfort and safety, flow with the changes. You will notice beliefs and judgments that lurked in the background of your psyche, coming front and center for your review and release. If these beliefs and judgments don't serve you, let them go gracefully.

I can tell you that it is possible to go through this transformation with grace and ease. Yet I have seen people go through it in much pain, kicking and screaming all the way. Understand that your discomfort will be in the areas where you resist letting go of that which does not serve your highest good.

Relationships, work situations, geographical location, and your body — everything will be subject to review. If it doesn't serve you, it's out of here. Surrender to your Divine Wisdom and let these forms go gracefully. Embrace the new people and opportunities that present themselves.

Thus, in August 2001, the *Sacred Union Program* was born. I used myself as a guinea pig along with a few brave friends. I experienced the Divine Birth in late August and it took a few months to integrate the new energy. The biggest thing I noticed was a huge decrease in self-judgment. This seemed to affect everything. In the absence of judgment, there is compassion and unconditional acceptance. All of my metaphysical powers increased dramatically. People told me that I looked younger and was radiating. I noticed that the new friends I was making were people who were much clearer and self-assured.

I manifested a home that certainly reflected my version of Paradise on Earth. It sat on a ridge overlooking a river canyon in Kaua'i. Directly across the canyon is a beautiful waterfall. Behind the waterfall is a sacred hill and behind that, beautiful mountains. Every morning a gorgeous sunrise view greeted me. The sound of the waterfall filled my home with constant music.

A Sacred Union Partner

In late October 2001, I initiated the fourth step and called for an intimate *Sacred Union Partner*. I summarized a six-page list of everything I wanted to manifest in a partner and in a partnership. Then with the help of some good friends, we did a ceremony and launched the manifestation. Here is what I asked for.

> My partner is open, his available heart ready, willing and able to make an intimate heart connection. His sense of humor tickles my heart and mind and demonstrates his intelligence and playfulness. He is a beautiful man — both inside and out. I love to caress him with my eyes and fingers. The chemistry between us is electrifying.
>
> He communicates clearly and fully. We communicate clearly and fully together. We have sooooo much fun. He lets love rule his mind and actions. His mission and mine are aligned and complimentary. He travels with me as I act as a Divine Midwife for Birthing the Divine Humans wherever the Divine Children call to me. We nourish each other in *Sacred Union* Partnership. He too, is an abundant being. He loves himself and me unconditionally. He is a man of courage and integrity, evolving into a Divine Human.
>
> My partner and I are playmates and we share a pure unconditional love, a deep sense of intimacy at all levels and profound sense of freedom in this relationship. When we are together we play and laugh a lot. We also spend quiet, blissful moments, just being. Our lovemaking is passionate, playful, free and deeply satisfying. He matches me energetically mentally, spiritually and emotionally. His male and female aspects are completely balanced, but most often he expresses himself as male energy in our relationship and allows me to express the feminine. Like me, he is an abundant being. His destiny and mine are aligned and we perform our service to the world together, which creates incredible synergy, contribution, prosperity, harmony, joy and fulfillment. This partnership nourishes us both. Our love is so pure; it is like touching the face of God.

Within a few days, my guidance told me that a man had been identified that matched my manifestation. I was told he didn't live on Kaua'i and was far away. My response was, "Well, get him here, then. People visit here from all over the world." The response from Spirit was, "You'll meet him before the end of the year."

Just to give my manifestation another shot of energy, I visualized my body as a huge lighthouse, sending out my light all over the world. I visualized my beloved as a sea captain who saw my light and followed it, sailing into my arms.

No more than six weeks later, I saw Casey for the first time. I had arrived early for a community meeting and decided to kill some time looking through a nearby tourist shop. As I walked up the stairs to the shop, a ruggedly handsome, bearded man, with electric blue eyes opened the door for me.

An electrical shock wave ran through my body that said, "Yes!" It was gone in an instant, but it had rocked me to my core. He sure looked like a sea captain. Could this be him? Self-doubt crept in immediately, telling me that he was probably a tourist and I would *never* see him again.

He hung around long enough to open the door for me as I exited the shop. His twinkling blue eyes focused on me intently, telling me that he liked what he was seeing. I smiled and nodded my thank you, passing him on my way to the meeting.

Never didn't last very long. After a few minutes Captain Blue Eyes showed up at the community meeting. The group leader asked us all to introduce ourselves. I learned that the sea captain was Casey Holt, a massage therapist, who moved to the island two weeks ago from St. Louis, Missouri.

Our eyes met from across the room and we held each other's gaze for so long it seemed like a stare. He had come to the meeting with a female friend who noticed our growing connection and ushered him away as fast as she could. We ran into each other several times in the following weeks, wordlessly weaving our energies. On December 23 we both showed up at the same holiday dance party.

It took him a painfully long time to peel himself from the wall and ask me to dance. I accepted with delight and we have been dancing together ever since. We shared our thoughts and feelings easily and completely. We played like little children, two new friends who couldn't get enough of each other.

At one point, about a week into our new acquaintance, I heard a voice within me say, "He is NOT the one you asked for." I could see that there were a few things on my wish list that he didn't embody. I asked for somebody who was free from addictions, and he smoked. I asked for someone who loved himself unconditionally, and he was tormented with self-judgment.

Yet, the connection was so deep, powerful, fun and juicy, I felt that if he wasn't the one I asked for, then he certainly was the one that was sent to help prepare the way for my true beloved. I decided to surrender into the joy of the "now" moment and not be concerned about how long the relationship would last.

In the year since I moved to Kaua'i, Kathy and Rod Russell, the *Trance Channel Team*, were personal friends and loving supporters. They were the core of my soul family and I often went to them when my emotional disharmony clouded my spiritual guidance. In a channeling, I asked Goddess Athena, who spoke through Rod, about my inner voice that said Casey wasn't *The One* I asked for.

She told me that he IS the one I manifested. She said that my inner voice told me what I needed to hear to relax into the relationship. If I had believed, early on, that he was *The One*, I would have put too much pressure on the relationship and he would have bolted. By telling myself he wasn't *The One*, I gave us both a chance to explore each other without any expectations.

He wasn't the one I asked for, yet he was the one I manifested. Both statements felt true, but on the surface, conflicting. Now I see how both statements were true at the same time. I wasn't quite ready for everything I had asked for because I manifested him before I had completely integrated my own *Sacred Union*. I manifested him to mirror the last little bit of woundedness I still needed to heal. Yet there couldn't be very much wounding left, because it felt so good to be with him.

David Deida's books, tapes and videos helped me get through this time with grace and ease. David teaches about the difference between male and female energy. He says that men's greatest fear is to lose their freedom, while women's greatest fear is to lose their love relationship. I realized how, in the past, when I sensed a man was pulling away from me emotionally, I would do something to try to pull him closer. To a man, this feels suffocating and they tend to pull away even more. I used what I learned from David Deida's materials to behave differently this time.

For the first six months we dove almost effortlessly into deeper and deeper levels of intimacy. Casey had been single for twelve years and had vowed to keep it that way. There were palpable moments when we would come to a point where we would each have to choose to go deeper or say goodbye. A pattern emerged where I would decide first to open to the next deeper level, realizing that Casey might decide to leave. I would hold a healthy state of detachment for a few days while he made his decision.

He consistently chose to go deeper with me until we got to the point where the next deepest level was living together. That is were he drew the line. Casey consistently told me, and everybody else, that he moved to Kaua'i to work on himself, by himself, and he didn't want to get involved in a relationship. I clearly and consistently told Casey that it was my intent to manifest a *Sacred Union Partnership*.

Though he expressed his love and honor for me in numerous non-verbal ways, he couldn't say, "I love you," and cringed every time I professed my love for him. Yet I told him anyway, vowing to myself, not to suppress my emotions for anybody.

We came to a difficult point. He wanted to keep things the way they were, spending five days a week together, yet not living together or making a deeper commitment. I longed for a *Sacred Union* and told myself that if this didn't work for him, then I needed to let him go and make space in my life for someone who wanted the same thing I did. How could we honor ourselves and honor each other too?

It was a very emotional and confusing time. We both sought a session with Kathy and Rod and the Ascended Masters that spoke through them. Casey's session was first and we agreed to meet at the beach in the hour between his appointment and mine.

A *Sacred Union* Partner

We arrived at the beach at the same time, coming from opposite directions. He ran to me, whipped off his sunglasses, and with tears in his eyes, told me for the first time, "Suzanna, I love you." I melted into his arms and spread kisses all over his face, our tears mingling. Then he continued to say it over and over again, as if the floodgates had opened and couldn't be contained any longer.

This went on for quite a few minutes and of course, I assumed that meant that whatever Kathy, Rod and Spirit had said to him, they assured him it was in his best interest to go deeper into relationship with me. In fact, that is what they advised.

Amidst the joy of love finally expressed, he told me that to honor himself; he was still choosing to go forward on his own without me. What I thought was a joyful union turned out to be a loving parting of the ways.

You can imagine the rollercoaster ride my emotional body went through in that hour. By the time I showed up at Kathy and Rod's for my appointment, I was a basket case. They were shocked to hear my news. They knew Spirit told him that it was in his highest good to enter into a partnership with me, but 'only if he wanted to be happy.' I guess happiness, for him, was an idea too foreign to even entertain.

We parted lovingly with respect and honor for each other. For the next three weeks, I grieved deeply, giving full expression to every emotion. At four weeks I came out of it feeling cleansed, acknowledging the gifts Casey gave me, the lessons learned and again ready to give love another chance.

I revised my *Sacred Union Partner* list and emphasized that I wanted somebody who was head-over-heels in love with me and not afraid to express it. I did another ceremony and launched my new manifestation. This time my guides told me that my match did live on the island and it would take them ten weeks to prepare him for me.

Now I felt confident I could manifest a partner and trust my inner voice. I happily waited out the ten weeks, knowing that being in the state of joy would open me to new love. I ran into Casey twice, both times, grateful that I felt a comfortable detachment and no pain in his presence. I was convinced that I had successfully released him and was ready for a new love to walk into my life.

Eight weeks into my waiting period, I got a phone call from a woman on Oahu who had seen one of my articles on the internet. She said she felt a connection to me and my work. In getting to know her, I found that she was very clairvoyant and had a gift for facilitating inner-child work over the phone. To give me a sample of her gift, she began reading my energy field and described some issues with my mother and father that needed release.

I gave her permission to facilitate a healing. With those issues released, she said a man immediately popped into my field. She described Casey to a T. She said that there was still some question about whether we were really done with each other or not. I told her I had manifested a new partner. But she said that Casey was so big in my field, that if somebody else was there, she couldn't see him. She said that we were not complete with each other and our wounded inner boys were mirrors for each other. She told me that if I didn't heal my inner child, I would just attract another man with a wounded inner child. She said I couldn't have a true *Sacred Union* relationship until this healing was complete.

Committed to my own *Sacred Union*, it didn't take me long to get on the phone with Casey and share what I had learned about our wounded inner boys. I presented my reasoning that since we loved, honored and trusted each other, we could facilitate a healing for each other. Then we could both be free to go our separate ways. I asked him if he would be willing to get back together for a little while for this specific purpose. He didn't hesitate to agree.

There have been many times in my life where I had to call upon my courage, but this seemed to take more than usual. I told myself that I had survived our separation before and for such a worthy cause, I could do it again. We proceeded cautiously at first, but then one night turned into five and we were in love even more deeply than before.

I wasn't aware of the moment it happened, how or why, but Casey finally realized that he could heal himself more quickly and more joyously within a relationship than without one. One day, I heard him introduce me as his partner and I just stared at him in amazement. By Fall Equinox, ten weeks, to the day, my new partner showed up. It was a new and improved Casey — head-over-heels in love with me and not afraid to express it.

In November 2002, almost a year since we met, Casey moved in with me and we performed a *Sacred Union* ceremony for ourselves. I find this relationship nurturing and nourishing. It is like no relationship I have had before. Our love is still growing and deepening in ways I never imagined.

The Eleventh Hour

In August 2002 I began facilitating the *Sacred Union Program* with individuals and groups here on the island and over the phone. It has become obvious that this is a very successful and potent program.

I counted on the *Sacred Union Program* to begin supporting me financially, hoping this new income stream would kick in, just in time before the money from the divorce settlement ran out. When I met Casey, he had just sold his home in St. Louis and had almost exactly the same amount in his bank account that I did. When he moved in, we shared all of our expenses equally.

Neither of us had a regular job but we both did our healing work as much as we could. This didn't bring in a significant income, so we lived off our savings. We trusted that any moment, our healing gifts would be recognized more fully in the world and would support us financially.

From time to time, my mind would tell me to "write the book," but I just couldn't make myself sit still long enough to accomplish anything. In September 2003 I began offering the *Sacred Union Program* using teleconference technology and this helped a lot. Even so, when November 2003 rolled around, the balance in both our bank accounts went below $1000 and things got scary.

February 2, 2004. Panic sets in. I've never been here before. All the money from the divorce settlement is gone. It supported me for six years, but now it's gone. The book still isn't finished. I paid this month's rent. I have finally taken a couple part time jobs; neither promises to make enough to pay next month's rent.

On this island paradise, there are no good-paying jobs. There is nothing comparable to the high-paying consulting work I used to do. I could work in a tourist shop, making $10 per hour; but not getting enough hours to make it add up to anything substantial. Even if I were offered 40 hours per week, that's only $400 and then with taxes taken out — not enough to survive. I could go into fear and panic. Sometimes I do. How did I get here?

Sacred Union: A Journey To Joyful Living

My expectations were that by the time the divorce settlement ran out, the *Sacred Union Program* would be attracting enough people to support me. *The Sacred Union Program* — such a gift to the world. The transformation is so profound, so all-encompassing. It seems like the keys to the kingdom and yet why aren't people recognizing that?

Now the judgments start coming. Am I not an effective messenger? Am I not an effective salesperson? If this technology is so great, why am I sitting here in poverty? What illusion have I been buying into? What have I done wrong? What have I not understood or remembered or practiced well enough?

What have I done wrong? I thought I was following the guidance. I thought I was listening to the small still voice within. I've totally believed the spiritual teachings and lived them. Was it all bull shit? Have I been lied to? Have I been lying to myself? Are there some malevolent forces that are working against me, blocking me from breaking through?

The manifesting principals worked so well for so long. I manifested the life I wanted and I lived it. Or was I living a lie? Because I had money in the bank as a safety net, did that mean I wasn't really walking my talk? Have I been abandoned? Have I abandoned myself? I thought I cleared all this. Wasn't the beautiful life I was leading proof that I had cleared it? What is happening? Confusion. Doubt. Fear.

It is the eleventh hour. It's 11:55. Something has to change fast. Is it my understanding? Is it my consciousness? Is it my beliefs? Is there something inside I still need to clear? Is it a door that opens? Is it an opportunity that presents itself just in the nick of time. Do all the seeds I've sown finally start sprouting?

I can't even believe I'm in this position. I started working when I was 15 and I've always had enough money to do what I wanted. My wants and desires haven't been that big. I never used to look at the price at the grocery store. I couldn't be bothered with coupons. It seemed that my karma, my consciousness, my frequency presented me with a life of grace and ease and comfort. What happened? Why did it change? Or did it?

Is this perceived lack an illusion? God, I hope so. I've been told we are in a new energy now. We are supposed to be in a new consciousness and a new level of Divinity where instant manifestation is supposed to be happening. We are supposed to be *Divine Human*s creating Paradise on Earth. I really believed that. I walked it. I talked it. I taught it to others and they believed me.

I believed we create our own reality — totally and completely. Why have I created this? Either it's true, or it's not. What a horrible possibility to entertain — that I've been wrong all along.

This is what I do when what I'm thinking makes me feel sick. I rationalize. I'm one of the best rationalizers around. Here it goes. I'm going to talk myself into feeling better.

Before I do, I have to back up just a few days. I was feeling quite desperate. Nothing seemed to be working or making sense. I decided that there might be something within me to clear, or something outside of me that was having a negative influence. I contacted a Galactic Counselor who has the ability to see into your Galactic Blueprint. This blueprint goes back to the beginning of when you where individualized as a Divine Spark. Casey and I asked if there was anything that needed clearing, healing and balancing that might be getting in the way of our ability to reach the people who we could serve with the gifts we had to share. We asked for anything that was blocking prosperity. I must say, we found quite a lot of obstacles.

For a fascinating hour, I listened to the counselor tell me who I am as a Galactic Citizen, and how my past acts, perceptions and beliefs were affecting my current life in this physical plane. We cleared, healed, balanced and received instructions for setting this right. We learned a great deal and our gratitude for this timely intervention is beyond human expression.

One of the things we learned was that when we moved to this island of Kaua'i, we had not followed protocol. Apparently we were supposed to present ourselves to the Kahuna Guardian of this island who is an ancestor in spirit form. The protocol is to present yourself and state your intentions and ask permission to live or work from here. It is customary to offer natural gifts such as fruit, flowers, leis, crystals, etc.

Sacred Union: A Journey To Joyful Living

From what I came to understand, even though the Spirit of Kaua'i, which I refer to as Mother Kaua'i, called us here and embraced us, protocol demanded that we clear it with her guardians as well. I wish I would have known this three years ago!

Yet, it seemed to make sense. From the spiritual and emotional standpoint (feminine characteristics), I did feel very nourished and nurtured living here. But from the physical, financial, masculine aspect, we were not being supported at all. Both Casey and I had savings that supported us for a few years, but with very little income being generated from our healing practices, of course, we ran out.

Casey and I went to the haeau (sacred Hawaiian Temple) at the mouth of the Wailua River and asked permission to enter the sacred space. We addressed the spirit Kahuna, his two generals, the devas, elementals and the volcano Goddess Pele'. We presented ourselves, our gift offerings and apologies for not showing up sooner. We asked permission to live and work from here as a home base. We explained the sacred service we hoped to share with the people of the island and the world. We gave praise and gratitude for the service that they were providing in guarding and taking care of the island. We asked them to support us in thriving here on Kaua'i.

I imagined they heard me, and based on the warm, fuzzy feelings I was having, I assumed they granted permission. I also got the idea that I needed to share my new understanding of the protocol with the many friends I had made on this island. There were many, who like me, felt called here by Mother Kaua'i, but weren't making it financially.

There was another friend and sister Priestess that helped me during this time, Gayle Newhouse. She helped clear away some blocks that had been placed around me by other healers who because of past-life jealously, subconsciously didn't want to see me share my work with the world. She helped me balance my emotional and energy bodies, and come into a place of inner peace and quiet. Then she helped me blast through the last of my abundance issues. Her incredible clairvoyance, compassion and groundedness were a tremendous support at a time when I was beginning to feel abandoned by humans and Spirit alike.

Assuming that my full powers of manifestation have been reinstated, I AM now free to manifest whatever I want. I went back to my computer files to find the script for my life that I had written in 1996. In reviewing it, I noticed that my dream hadn't changed much. It seemed like most of the dream had already come true. The missing link, what I hadn't manifested yet, was "The Book" and the income that supported the life I loved.

I relaunched my manifestation, rededicating myself to my own vision. Just like the first time, the universe responded immediately. Ideas started coming in for new teleclasses to offer. New avenues for advertising my teleclasses were suggested and people in the business world started being attracted to my offerings. I also attracted a few new people who were so impressed with the *Sacred Union Program* they began referring clients to me.

Casey got a job and was feeling better about having a steady paycheck. His massage business opened up to include referrals from a doctor.

It wasn't a get-rich-quick situation, but enough money was flowing in to keep up with expenses. The biggest difference was that we let go of fear and trusted that our Divine Selves knew what we needed and would provide it. This opening to trust seemed to open the cash flow. WOW! That was a close call.

In the past year, I have opened to new spiritual initiations, raising my frequency and expanding my consciousness once more. I am learning what it means to be a *Divine Human* in Mastery. I am learning that there is a technical side to this Ascension Business and the relationship between ascension upgrades and initiations. I've been learning that *Sacred Union* is not a program, but is a state of consciousness that can be hosted by *Divine Human*s on this planet.

Casey and I were married on Valentine's Day, 2005. Instead of the traditional wedding vows, we vowed to anchor and express the Paradise Blueprint and energy through us for the benefit of all. We are two *Divine Humans*, consecrating our creative energy to the Divine Plan of Heaven on Earth.

Creating Sacred Inner Space

Pillar of Light

Let's begin by taking some long, deep breaths. Imagine, just pretend, that you are breathing in through the top of your head and breathing out through the bottom of your feet. You will use the imagination as a tool to direct energy. The energy will flow where your attention goes. Inhale through the top of your head, exhale through the bottom of your feet.

Call now to the Source of All That Is, the Great Central Sun to send down a beam of white light. It comes in through the top of your head the moves all the way through your body and out through the bottom of your feet. Then it continues down through all the layers of the Earth until it reaches the Heart of Mother Earth and anchors at the crystal core there.

As Mother Earth feels this beam of light enter her heart, she smiles. She responds by sending up here own loving beam of light — a ruby-red light of vibrant, passionate life-force energy. This energy passes up through the layers of Earth, passing all the way through your body and continuing on into the very heart of Source.

So now you have two beams of light, one white and one ruby-red anchored in the Heart of Source and anchored in the Heart of Mother Earth as they pass through you. These two beams of light begin dancing together, dancing together, dancing together and now merging together in *Sacred Union.*

As these two energies merge together, creating a new energy. The synergy of this new energy expands the light outward in all directions, filling up your body. It expands again to fill up your energy field, and expands again to fill up size of the room you are in. Acknowledge the energy, the vibration of grace. It has a rose quartz color and texture. Grace is the name of the frequency of light that allows us to let go of that which no longer serves us, easily and gracefully. It also allows us to take quantum leaps in our evolution easily and gracefully, just by setting the intention for transformation, and then gracefully allowing it to unfold in its own sacred time.

Sphere of Compassion

Now surround yourself with a safe and sacred space for transformation to happen. Imagine and create a sphere that is the size of your room. The walls of the sphere are made up of spheres within spheres — trillions of them. Anywhere you look on the wall of the big room-size sphere, a smaller whole and complete sphere exists. This is called a sphere hologram. The room-size sphere and all the little spheres that make up the wall are all spinning at the speed, at the frequency, of unconditional love. It is the highest frequency in the universe, the vibration of compassion.

Become aware that within the walls of this sphere, anything that vibrates at a frequency less than compassion cannot enter this space. Also become aware that this sphere is programmed to automatically go back to the Source of All That Is after this session. Anything that is released into this sphere will be transmuted and purified and available for reassignment by Source.

So you are beginning to feel the vibration of compassion as it permeates your energy field and saturates your cells. Feel this energy as it enters your heart center and opens the emotional heart. You are becoming aware that you benefit most from the gifts of Spirit when your hearts is open. You know that this a completely safe place to open and allow yourself to receive.

Star of David

Turn your attention back to the Sphere of Compassion. Become aware that in Sacred Geometry, the sphere contains all other sacred forms within it. Today call upon the sacred form called the Star of David to come forth from the walls of the sphere and superimpose itself right on top of your body. The Star of David has been acknowledged for its power since ancient times as a sacred symbol. It contains two triangles, one pointing up and one point down. They are superimposed on each other. Now the triangle, in sacred geometry is known as a portal. It is a doorway through which spiritual energy enters matter. That is why the pyramids are made up of triangles. Energy from Source enters the Earth through these triangles. So with the Star of David, you have a very focused portal of energy.

Notice the point of the star that is about a foot above your head — this contains the pink flame of unconditional love. Feel the vibration of this flame of love as it is ignited and burns softly above your head. Maybe with your mind's eye you can see it.

Notice the point of the star that is about a foot to the right of your right hip. This contains the yellow flame of Divine Wisdom. Feel; imagine the energy of this flame.

Move your attention to the point of the star that is about a foot to the left of your left hip — this contains the blue flame of Divine Power, Divine Will. Experience the energy of this flame for a moment. So that was the triangle that points up. Now move your attention to the triangle that points down.

Notice the golden ray in the point of the star about a foot to the right of your right shoulder. This golden ray comes from the masculine aspect of Source, from the Great Central Sun.

In the point of the star to the right of your right shoulder, we have the platinum ray, coming from the feminine aspect if Source in the Great Central Moon. In the point of the star about a foot below the base of your spine, we have the ruby-red ray of Mother Earth. She anchors this Star of David into your energy field and into the Earth.

Now notice that the beautifully colored flames and rays in the points of the star are moving into the middle of the star, in the middle of your body, dancing together, dancing together, dancing together and now merging together in *Sacred Union*. Acknowledge the synergy when these six light frequencies merge and create a new vibration. This is the energy field that you will bask in during your transformation.

Testimonials

"As a student of the Metaphysical for 34 years, a certified Hypnotherapist, a psychic and a light worker, I've read tons of books and studied many various practices in search of Enlightenment. Haven't we all?

I've had lots of "Ah-ha's", pieces and whole sections of the Grand puzzle gathered and filed away in my mind. But I could never quite see the whole picture, or how I fit into it. I just never hit on a sure fire, step-by-step method that made sense. Now I have.

Six months ago, a close friend of mine began a new program channeled through a woman in Hawaii. My friend raved about it, and each week that passed, I watched her shift old patterns, heal, grow. Yes, I was impressed but I kept thinking to myself "Been there, done that, got the T-shirt". Then she made a major life change. She let go of an obsessive relationship that had been haunting her since she was 18. The one that I had been counseling her on for years and getting nowhere. And she just let it go. Now I was really impressed. I signed up for the program.

Sacred Union by Suzanna Kennedy really works. It is, in my opinion, the perfect blend of psychology, hypnosis, guided meditation and spirituality, (with the emphasis on Spirit). I plan on taking the facilitator training so that I can help my loved ones become conscious of their *Divine Human*ity.

Since every person who raises their frequency also raises the frequency of the planet and the Universe, I believe it is the 'job' of every healer/teacher to do what they can to assist in this. I believe that the *Sacred Union Program* is a gift to that end."

Christine Nelson
Horton, Michigan

"Years of guilt. Years of self-dislike. Years of being a workaholic. Years of denying my feminine side. Years of self-denial. Gone. How sweet it is. Of course, it took work. It had the "peeling-the-onion" quality. With each "peeling," new stuff pops up. Then I used Suzanna's approaches to clear the issues and bring in the new energies.

Appendix

*Sacred Union*s — that's scary stuff. Relationships — been there, done that, leave it on the shelf. But I used the Divine Discipline a few months ago (because I didn't want to be the only holdout) to identify my Divine Partner. (Yeah, right!) And two months later, he showed up!

Suzanna's gentle guidance and effective facilitation techniques have transformed so many, and positively impacted the Earth. I've watched her every step of the way: from her first visit to Sedona, to her "summer assignment" in Arizona," to her move to Hawaii. This book represents only part of her work — and it is truly remarkable."

Kathy Lowe
Sedona, Arizona

"When I attended a *Sacred Union* Playshop with Suzanna, I had a profound experience and immediately it began to change my life, for the better. That is why I signed up to take the Teleclass Series. I admit that I was skeptical at first about whether it would be as effective over the phone. But for me, the teleclass was even more profound. At the playshop, if anyone would move or cough, it would pull me a little bit out of the depth of the experience. It was a little hard to completely relax in the group. I found that when we did this on the phone, I could still feel the energy of the group, but because I was in my own home, I could relax completely and went much deeper and had an even more profound experience. With Suzanna's voice in my ear, I felt that she was so close to me, even closer than in the playshop. I felt her in my aura.

We have completed the series now and I feel so at peace within myself. Things that used to bother me don't anymore. It feels easier for me to speak my truth. I finally feel free to express myself. I look at my life from a new, higher level of awareness. I understand why things are the way they are. I am receiving very clear guidance from my Inner Advisors. I am releasing fear from my consciousness. Everything is more joyful to me."

Anna Verbich
Clayton, California

"The *Sacred Union Program* worked for me because I was open to it. I was ready for change. The *Sacred Union* Technology

203

and Suzanna's facilitation guided me and helped me to complete what my heart was longing for. Suzanna is a very gifted communicator and her soft tone of her voice was very pleasant and easy to listen to."

"During the session I was enveloped in this loving energy. A consciousness that was me, opened to me, and revealed the fact that I'm not just this person that I know myself to be — that I can be more. It welcomed me to take the journey to be more. It flowed and evolved to the point where I feel joy and peace and love."

"What I would like people to know is that the *Sacred Union Program* is available. And **you too** can feel loved, needed and purposeful."

Ana Zach
Princeville, Hawaii

"What drew me to the *Sacred Union Program* was the comprehensive nature of the process. Every step builds on the previous one and in the end, the changes you have are permanent. Sometimes you go to a workshop and have a temporary high. Then you go back home and to work and it goes back to what it was before. With this, the change of experience is permanent."

"For me, Suzanna has been a great Spiritual Midwife. She was always there when I was working through temporary difficulties and was ready to celebrate the positive changes as they came in. I feel really grateful for her bringing this process through and putting it in a format that is easily accessible to all of us."

"I found the *Sacred Union* Technology to be very simple and very easy and very, very powerful." The sessions themselves were a beautiful experience. It felt safe at all times and I was comfortable because every step appeared to be activated through my conscious participation. The energy was set up and built during the session and it felt very loving and powerful."

"People have to be very clear about what they are asking for (after taking the *Sacred Union Program*) because in my experience, not only are you going to get it, but you will get it real fast. And we are not used to that."

Siglinde Schwenzl

Appendix

Kaua'i, Hawaii

"As my friendship with Suzanna developed and deepened, I became acutely aware of her integrity and the time she spent in developing this program. This peaked my interest and made me want to take part in it for myself. It's very simple, yet it hits at the core issues that I knew I needed in order to develop myself."

"Suzanna is a powerful and professional facilitator. It is evident that she has put many years of work into this. She makes transformation very easy and very gentle. It was a very simple procedure and one that was very peaceful."

"I would like people to know how simple this program is and how powerful it is. It reaches to the core issues that are universal to all of us."

Ceci Connor
Makawao, Hawaii

"Thank you seems so insignificant for this great gift of completion of the *Sacred Union Program* with Suzanna Kennedy, who is an exceptional model of *Sacred Union*. I enjoy being who I am for the first time in my life. During the process of the *Sacred Union Program*, my experiences were many and diverse, however, the following are the most prominent that I remember.

Detoxifying

Since joining the *Sacred Union Program*, I have been continually detoxifying and releasing energies that no longer serve me. I feel like I'm working on a new body that is a bridge towards higher consciousness. The toxins being released are too numerous to mention. I could feel the release through the sweat glands and pores of the skin as I bathed. Often, I had diarrhea after the meditations, as my body purged the negative blockages.

Body Aches & Pains

As my body transforms, I feel the old dissolving, while I give birth to the new me. Since I am sensitive, this can be a particularly uncomfortable experience. My body aches and pains are especially noticeable in the region of my left knee, back and head. The act of walking, exercising and stretching helps to move the energetic blockages, allowing the pain to be eased. I have learned to be present in my body and face the aches and pain by being in the moment. The more that I am in my body, the more alert and aware I become of my spiritual self.

Inner Peace

The removal of debris, baggage and old beliefs, has allowed me to blossom into the artist that I am. The biggest changes I've noticed are the inner peace, balance, and more self-love. The quiet, peaceful feeling inside me, without all of that chatter, is wonderful. "To bring peace to the earth, I strive to make my own life peaceful." Following each session, I always felt at peace and energized.

Before starting my spiritual quest including the *Sacred Union Program*, I felt separation from Source and my spiritual self. Following the program, it feels natural to check in each morning. I have conversations with my Spiritual Self and discuss future plans. I'm so much more connected to Source and myself than I have ever been. It's wonderful and I'm so grateful.

The critic was always present before the process, with opinions about everything and everybody, whether I wanted one or not. Now the inner critic is gone. This is especially important when working creatively.

As I continued with the program, I began to realize how many patterns I was carrying that belonged to my parents. The energy that comes down the family lines, as well as the culture and organized religion beliefs seemed to be a big part of the old beliefs.

Over the years I heard and read these spiritual concepts many times. However with this powerful *Sacred Union Program*, I was able to anchor the beliefs into my consciousness with the exercises and meditation with Suzanna. I am so grateful for the positive changes. This tends to make me believe there were a lot of unconscious beliefs being released.

With each exercise I experienced healing, integrating and transforming on so many levels: body, mind, spirit, and especially emotions. It was an inside cleansing as I've never felt before with big results. I have experienced more inner peace, harmony, and balance in my life since completing this program. With each session, I would feel more empowered, focused, and energized.

There were two conscious practices that helped me embody my spiritual self:

- Grounding my body into the earth is invaluable in discharging the excess and negative psychic energies that I picked up from others and the environment.

- Centering my awareness behind my eyes in the 6th chakra is my way of putting myself in a higher consciousness whenever I feel astray.

I am different within myself in so many ways, here are just a few:

- I feel more self-acceptance and self-love as I've worked through the *Sacred Union Program*.

- Creativity and spirituality are indistinguishable for me. Artistic expression is an interior process, as well as an exterior one. I feel more committed to a creative life and maintaining this inner/outer balance.

- Realizing now that I am a compassionate artist with a soul mission is important to me.

- By connecting with my spiritual self, I will help others awaken to their own gifts. "

Pamela Howett
Walnut Creek, CA

Resources

Adam El David, *Integrative Natural Healing*. Visit his website at www.iammahatma.com.

Alton Kamadon, *Melchizedek Method*. Visit his website at www.melchizedekmethod.com.

Diana James, *Academie of Sacred Aromatics*, Santa Fe, NM. Phone: 505.986.8887.

Vanda Osmon, *Joy Travel*, visit her website at www.joytravelonline.com.

Dr. Ann West, host of *Truth from the Source* on KKCR public radio. Visit her website at www.drannwest.com.

Rod and Kathy Russell, *Trance Channeling Team*. Private sessions in person on Kaua'i or over the phone. Check out their website at www.allowlove.com.

David Deida, teacher and author focusing on male-female energy within intimate relationships. Visit his website at www.bluetruth.org.

Jeanne Nicholson, *Sacred Union* Facilitator, Author, Healer, Spiritual Counselor. Visit her website at www.madamzelda.org. Phone: 248.478.8492.

Rev. Sandie Hall, Galactic Counselor, Teacher, Healer. Visit her website at www.galacticsolutions.com.

Gayle Newhouse, supports Masters, both embodied and in Spirit. She facilitates soul retrievals for individuals and for Mother Earth. Phone 808.652.1280.

Elyse Hope Killoran, Prosperity Teacher. Visit her website at www.choosingprosperity.com.

Business Training for Entrepreneurs, Shared Vision Network. Visit their website at www.sharedvisionnetwork.com.

Bryan DeFlores, Golden Age Business Plan, accelerator, artist www.bryandeflores.com.

Products and Services

Book *Sacred Union: A Journey To Sacred Union*
Self-Study Kit: *Divine Human Upgrades* Book, 10 CDs
Teleclass: *Divine Human Upgrades* 8 sessions plus Self-Study Kit
Private Sessions With Suzanna
CDs
■   Energy Medicine
■   Forgiving Yourself and Others
■   Manifesting From The Heart
■   Introduction To Divine Human Upgrades
DVD: *Introduction To Sacred Union* Dr. Ann West of Truth From The Source interviews Suzanna Kennedy, 45 minutes

Call or visit website for current prices

Order Options

Call Toll Free: 866.393.9001 or Direct at 808.821-1393

On-line at www.realitycrafting.com/products.htm

Fax: 866.363.6722
Email: sacredunion@realitycrafting.com

Made in the USA
Lexington, KY
10 November 2012